CHILDREN AS READERS IN CHILDREN'S LITERATURE

We are fascinated by text and we are fascinated by reading. Is this because we are in a time of textual change? Given that young people always seem to be in the vanguard of technological change, questions about what and how they read are the subject of intense debate. *Children as Readers in Children's Literature* explores these questions by looking at the literature that is written for children and young people to see what it tells us about them as readers. The contributors to this book are a group of distinguished children's literature scholars, literacy and media specialists who contemplate the multiple images of children as readers and how they reflect the power and purpose of texts and literacy.

Contributors to this wide-ranging text consider:

- How books shape the readers we become
- Cognitive and affective responses to representation of books and reading
- The relationship between love-stories and reading as a cultural activity
- Reading as 'protection and enlightenment'
- Picturebooks as stage sets for acts of reading
- Readers' perceptions of a writer.

This portrayal of books and reading also reveals adults' beliefs about childhood and literacy and how they are changing. It is a theme of crucial significance in the shaping of future generations of readers given these beliefs influence not only ideas about the teaching of literature but also about the role of digital technologies. This text is a must-read for any individual interested in the importance of keeping literature alive through reading.

Evelyn Arizpe is a Senior Lecturer at the School of Education, University of Glasgow, UK.

Vivienne Smith is Lecturer in the School of Education at the University of Strathclyde, UK.

CHILDREN AS READERS IN CHILDREN'S LITERATURE

The power of texts and
the importance of reading

Edited by Evelyn Arizpe and Vivienne Smith

Routledge
Taylor & Francis Group

LONDON AND NEW YORK

First published 2016
by Routledge
2 Park Square, Milton Park, Abingdon, Oxon OX14 4RN

and by Routledge
711 Third Avenue, New York, NY 10017

Routledge is an imprint of the Taylor & Francis Group, an informa business

British Library Cataloguing in Publication Data
A catalogue record for this book is available from the British Library

Library of Congress Cataloging in Publication Data
Children as readers in children's literature : the power of texts and the
importance of reading / edited by Evelyn Arizpe and Vivienne Smith.
pages cm
1. Children–Books and reading. 2. Teenagers–Books and reading. 3. Books
and reading in literature. 4. Books and reading–Psychological aspects.
5. Children's literature–History and criticism. 6. Young adult literature–
History and criticism. I. Arizpe, Evelyn, 1965- editor. II. Smith, Vivienne
(Teacher), editor.
Z1037.A1C465 2016
028.5'5–dc23
2015015006

ISBN: 978-1-138-80669-6 (hbk)
ISBN: 978-1-138-80670-2 (pbk)
ISBN: 978-1-315-75154-2 (ebk)

Typeset in Bembo
by Cenveo Publisher Services

CONTENTS

CONTRIBUTORS

Evelyn Arizpe is a Senior Lecturer at the School of Education, University of Glasgow, where she coordinates the MEd Programme in Children's Literature and Literacies. She has taught and published widely in the areas of literacy and children's literature and presented conference papers and keynote addresses at major international conferences. Evelyn has worked on a number of studies related to picturebooks and response, involving both children and adolescents; the most recent was the international research project *Visual Journeys through Wordless Narratives* on the responses of immigrant children to Shaun Tan's wordless narrative, *The Arrival* (Arizpe, E., Colomer, T. and Martínez-Roldán, C. Bloomsbury Academic, 2014). Her research team won the 2013 BERA Award for University/School research collaboration for the Esmée Fairbairn Foundation funded project *Journeys from Images to Words*. Currently, with Morag Styles, she is preparing a new edition of *Children Reading Pictures: Interpreting Visual Texts* (Routledge, forthcoming 2015).

Julia Eccleshare is the Children's Books Editor of the Guardian, editorial consultant for Lovereading4kids and a regular commentator on radio and at literary festivals. In addition to chairing the judges of the Guardian Children's Book Prize she has judged numerous prizes and is the founder and chair of the Branford Boase Award. Her books include *A Guide to the Harry Potter Novels, Beatrix Potter to Harry Potter: Portraits of Children's Writers, The Rough Guide to Teenage Books, The Rough Guide to Picture Books* and *1001 Children's Books to Read before You Grow Up*. She was presented with the Eleanor Farjeon Award in 2000 in recognition of her outstanding contribution to children's books. She was appointed MBE for services to children's literature, 2014 and received a DLitt (Hons) from the University of Worcester, 2014.

Maureen A. Farrell is a Senior Lecturer at the School of Education, University of Glasgow. She was previously an English teacher before moving into Higher

Education and teacher education in particular. Maureen contributes to the language courses for both primary and secondary teachers in degree and Masters programmes at the university as well as being a key team member on the successful MEd Children's Literature and Literacy Programme. Maureen has a particular interest in Scottish children's literature and has published work in this area: she is currently co-editing a book on this topic. She was a member of the international research project *Visual Journeys* and was involved with the follow up project *Journeys from Images to Words*, an award-winning project funded by the Esmée Fairbairn Foundation. She is also interested in picturebooks, graphic novels and the emerging field of digital books including book apps.

Shirley Brice Heath is Margery Bailey Professor of English and Dramatic Literature and Professor of Linguistics, Emerita, Stanford University. For more than three decades she has led ground-breaking research on overlaps in the learning environments of science laboratories, and the rehearsal zones and studios of all the arts. As a linguistic anthropologist, she has spent extensive time in these environments, recording language, uses of props and gestures, and reliance on visual discernment and movements of the hand and forearm. She has written extensively about children's literature and play, analysing changes over decades in relation to shifts in parental work patterns and valuation of entertainment for children as distinct from play and work projects with adults. She has published more than a dozen books, 200 articles and directed several documentary films portraying young people working in the arts.

Peter Hunt is Professor Emeritus in English and Children's Literature at Cardiff University. He has lectured on Children's Literature at more than 150 universities, colleges and to learned societies in 23 countries, has written or edited 26 books on the subject and more than 500 papers and reviews. His books have been translated into Arabic, Chinese, Danish, Greek, Japanese, Korean, Persian, Portuguese (Brazil) and Serbian. His latest work includes the children's literature section of *Oxford Online Bibliographies* (OUP New York, 2013), a collection of essays on Tolkien (Palgrave, 2013) and (with Dennis Butts) *How Did Long John Silver Lose his Leg, and 26 Other Mysteries of Children's Literature* (Lutterworth, 2013). He has also written six books for children and teenagers, including *Backtrack* (1986). In 2003 he was awarded the Brothers Grimm Award for services to children's literature, from the International Institute for Children's Literature, Osaka.

Maria Nikolajeva is a Professor of Children's Literature at the Faculty of Education, University of Cambridge, and the director of the Cambridge Research and Teaching Centre for Children's Literature. She is the author and editor of numerous books, including *Power, Voice and Subjectivity in Literature for Young Readers* (2010) and *Reading for Learning: Cognitive Approaches to Children's Literature* (2014). In 2005 she received the International Grimm Award for a lifetime achievement in children's literature research.

Kimberley Reynolds is the Professor of Children's Literature in the School of English Literature, Language and Linguistics at Newcastle University in the UK. Recent publications include an audio book, *Children's Literature between the Covers* (Modern Scholar, 2011), and *Children's Literature* in the Oxford University series of Very Short Introductions (2012). In 2013 she received the International Brothers Grimm Award for her contributions to the field of children's literature research. She has recently completed a monograph titled *Left Out: The Forgotten Radical Tradition of Publishing for Children in Britain, 1910–1949* (Oxford University Press, 2016).

Vivienne Smith lectures in Primary Education at the University of Strathclyde. Her interests are in language, literacy and literature and she has published on the development of children as readers, on comprehension and on children's literature. She is particularly interested in the way that the best texts encourage readers to reflect on their lives, their thinking and on reading itself. Significant publications include 'Words and Pictures: Towards a Linguistic Understanding of Picture Books and Reading Pedagogy', in S. Ellis and E. McCartney (Eds.), *Applied Linguistics in The Primary School* (Cambridge University Press, 2010); 'Comprehension as a Social Act: Texts, Contexts and Readers', in S. Ellis, U. Goswami, K. Hall, C. Harrison and J. Soler (Eds.), *Interdisciplinary Perspectives on Learning to Read* (Routledge, 2010) and 'Learning to be a Reader: Promoting Good Textual Health', in P. Goodwin (Ed.), *Understanding Children's Books* (Sage, 2008).

Morag Styles has recently retired as Professor of Children's Poetry at the Faculty of Education, Cambridge, and is an Emeritus Fellow of Homerton College. Morag is the author of numerous books and articles including, *From the Garden to the Street: 300 Years of Poetry for Children* (1998); co-author (with Evelyn Arizpe) of *Children Reading Pictures: Interpreting Visual Texts* (2003) and *Reading Lessons from the Eighteenth Century: Mothers, children and texts* (2006); co-editor of *Poetry and Childhood* (2009) and *Teaching Caribbean Poetry* (2013). She curated (with Michael Rosen) an exhibition on the history of children's poetry for the British Library in 2009. She is director of a Caribbean Poetry Project, a collaboration with The University of the West Indies.

Sylvia Warnecke was born and raised in the former German Democratic Republic, where she studied German and English at the Martin-Luther-Universität Halle/ Wittenberg, a renowned centre for children's literature studies at the time. In 1995 she moved to Scotland and lectured at the universities of Strathclyde, Heriot Watt and Stirling. In 1999, she graduated at the University of Manchester with a doctoral thesis on re-tellings of myths and ideology in GDR children's literature. Since 2003 Sylvia has been lecturing in German and later children's literature at the British Open University. In recent years her research has focused on adaptation as well as changes in reading fictions and meaning making in children's literature due to the advances in and impact of digital technologies.

Jean Webb is Professor of International Children's Literature and Director of the International Forum for Research in Children's Literature at the University of Worcester. Her publications include: Cogan Thacker, Deborah and Webb, Jean, *Introducing Children's Literature: Romanticism to Postmodernism* (Routledge, 2002); Jean Webb (Ed.) *'A Noble Unrest': Contemporary Essays on the Work of George MacDonald* (Cambridge Scholars Press, 2007); 'A.A. Milne's Poetic World of Childhood in *When We Were Very Young* and *Now We Are Six*', in M. Styles, L. Joy and D. Whitley (Eds.), *Poetry and Childhood* (Trentham, 2010); 'Picture Books and Multiple Readings: *When We Lived in Uncle's Hat* by Peter Stamm and Jutta Bauer', in E. Arizpe, M. Farrell and J. McAdam (Eds.), *Picturebooks Beyond the Borders of Art, Narrative and Culture* (Routledge, 2013); 'Food: Changing Approaches to Food in the Construction of Childhood in Western Culture', in Y. Wu, K. Mallan, R. McGillis (Eds.), *(Re)imagining the World: Children's Literature's Response to Changing Times* (Springer, 2013).

Mary Anne Wolpert is an Affiliated Lecturer at the Faculty of Education, University of Cambridge, and a Bye-Fellow of Homerton College. She is Primary PGCE Deputy Course Manager at the Faculty and has been a member of the research staff team for the Cambridge/Homerton Research and Teaching Centre for Children's Literature since its inception. She is a member of the advisory panels for the Children's Poetry Archive and a Caribbean Poetry Project, a collaboration with The University of the West Indies. Publications include chapters in *Teaching English Language and Literacy* (Wyse *et al.*, 2013), *Reflective Teaching* (Pollard *et al.*, 2014) and a contribution to a chapter in L. R. Sipe and S. Pantaleo (Eds.), *Postmodern Picturebooks; Play, Parody and Self-referentiality* (Routledge, 2008).

INTRODUCTION: THE FICTIONAL PORTRAYAL OF READING

Paradox and change

Vivienne Smith and Evelyn Arizpe

The context

We live in an age that is almost certainly more literate than any age has ever been before. In the developed world, and in many developing countries too, text is everywhere. It is in books and newspapers and magazines; it is wrapped around our food and our household necessities; it orders our communities with street signs and noticeboards, and tempts us in advertisements on hoardings and bus stops. These days, too, we have text on screens. Electronic displays tell us which train to catch, how to navigate our way through public buildings, when the next bus is due and even how to drive safely on the motorway. We carry electronic words everywhere. The work that once stayed in the office on our computers now travels with us on our own personal tablets and smartphones, and e-readers. And, even if the words and idioms are unrecognisable to the older generations, written text in the form of messages, tweets and 'posts' are now an inseparable part of the lives of younger generations.

We are fascinated by text. It is so much part of our everyday lives that we cannot envisage living without it. We depend on it in our work lives, our family lives and our social lives. Text gets things done. Text builds and maintains relationships. Text helps us think and text enables us to relax.

And, because we are fascinated by text, we are also fascinated by reading. For years there have been adult texts about reading. Italo Calvino's *If on a Winter's Night a Traveller* (1979), Umberto Eco's *The Name of the Rose* (1980), Orhan Pamuk's *The New Life* (1994), Douglas Adams' *The Hitchhiker's Guide to the Galaxy* (1979), are just some of those that have become famous. But now, in the early twentieth century, there seem to be even more of these books. *The Library of Shadows* by Mikkel Birkegaard (2007), *The Shadow of the Wind* by Carlos Ruiz Zafón (2001) and *Mr Penumbra's 24-Hour Bookstore* by Robin Sloan (2012) are best-selling examples.

Is this because we are in a time of textual change? Perhaps, as we swap our paperbacks for e-readers, we are confronted with the physicality of our own reading, and we reflect on how we read and why we read and what reading does for us. Increasingly, it seems, we read books and watch films about reading too. Bernhard Schlink's *The Reader* (1995), and the subsequent movie (2008), is an interesting example of the sort of text that has become popular in recent years. The story it tells of the concentration camp guard and the boy who befriends her might well have moved us at any time, but what gives the novel poignancy today is the examination of the disabling nature of Hanna's illiteracy and the curative effect of her subsequent flowering as a reader. It chimes with the way we want to think about reading. It shows us the best that reading can do and makes us anxious about what might possibly be lost if literacy practices change. Might we, in this increasingly fast, electronic world be moving away from literature?

Given that young people always seem to be in the vanguard of technological change, questions about literature and new literacies become increasingly pertinent and are the subject of intense debate. Are young people too busy updating their Facebook profiles to read literature? Are we nurturing a generation of grasshopper minds that lack the stamina to engage with the complex ideas and emotions that the best novels explore? In this highly literate world, are our young people less literate than previous generations? It seemed to us that one way to explore these questions would be to look at the literature that is written for children and for young people and see what that tells us about how we think of them as readers. In particular, we wanted to look at the way that reading is *shown*; what do the characters who read in children's books tell us about the way we conceptualise reading, and what might the real children who read these texts make of it?

This book, *Children as Readers in Children's Literature: The power of text and the importance of reading*, is the result of a series of workshops and a small conference at the University of Glasgow funded by the British Academy and called 'Reading Fictions'. In it scholars, all of whom were part of the workshop series, reflect on texts of their own choosing which have been written for children or young people and that seem to them to have something significant to say about the way reading has been shown or about how readers need to think as they read. Some of these texts are very recent and some are older, reaching back as far as the eighteenth century. Together they provide an overview of the way we, in the western world at least, have presented reading to our young over several generations.

Themes and paradoxes

What is always interesting about open-ended projects such as this is to watch as themes emerge, and here, despite (or perhaps because of) the variety of contributions and the range of texts we selected, concurrences and paradoxes have surprised and delighted us. They have confirmed us in our thinking and have made us reconsider.

Change, inevitably, is a major theme. We are amused to note the lack of change in many texts. So, for example, despite the obvious rise of electronic literacy in lives of both readers and authors of children's books, computers, e-readers and mobile phones rarely appear in children's literature. This is especially true in books for the very young. Some years ago, Jackie Marsh, as part of her research into very young children's engagement with new technologies (Marsh 2010) carried out a survey of the books in an infant classroom. She looked for images of any electronic technology: computers, games consoles, mobile phones, etc. She found very few: images of children pointing at a computer screen were as far as it went. More than five years on, we found that images of technology are still hard to find, though books featuring *books* have become increasingly common. There seems to be a fashion, for example, for books about bedtime stories (*Again!*, Gravett 2013 [2011]; *Dragon Loves Penguin*, Gliori 2013; *The Snatchabook*, Docherty and Docherty 2013). Where electronic devices are shown in picturebooks, the affordances are not always positive. Wolpert and Styles (Chapter 9) describe Lane Smith's *It's a Book* (2011 [2010]). They show how it positions reading the physical book as a more imaginative and engaging option than the tablet, even though, of course, it is perfectly possible to read the text of *Treasure Island* in either format. Zuckerberg and Berger's *Dot.* (2013) is another example. Dot is a child who spends too much time on her various electronic screens. They exhaust her. She needs to 'recharge, reboot and restart'. She does this by going out to play with her friends in the sunshine, and painting. What are we to make of this? Are we to deduce that technology is stifling her energy and creativity and turning her into a loner? It seems so.

What appears to be happening in all these texts is a re-manifestation of the romantic ideal of childhood. We see electronic literacy as a threat to the innocence of the child, who we think in our hearts should be frolicking in Hundred Acre Wood with Christopher Robin and Winnie-the-Pooh. Thus, the book itself, the artefact not the content, has become a symbol for what we want childhood to be.

The irony of this position is obvious, especially when we consider Nikolajeva's chapter (Chapter 1). She reminds us how, over a hundred years ago, it was reading *per se* that threatened to compromise Heidi's health and innocence. Drawing on a number of feisty (and mostly female) protagonists, she exposes a strong thread of resistance to reading that has existed from the very beginning of children's literature in the texts themselves. Reading, it appears, as well as being what authors want children to do to (especially when it comes to their own books) paradoxically sullies the soul, over stimulates the imagination and is plain unnecessary to a fulfilling life. Is this a legacy from earlier days when women were discouraged from reading for fear it would damage their moral, mental and physical health (Pearson 1999) or does it go even further back, to Don Quixote and all those bookworms who have been considered fools?

Alberto Manguel writes about the 'Book Fool', someone who devours books and ends up by confusing reality and fiction (2013). In his study of metaphors about readers, Manguel further identifies 'a deep, dark unease: the mistrust societies have always had toward that which can be created out of words ...' (p. 98). Does this mistrust include children's books? In the early twenty-first century, we who generally position reading as a good thing, find the association of mistrust (or foolishness) with books written for children very odd. Do Manguel's words reveal tension and an ambivalence in our attitudes towards children's reading that is rarely acknowledged? Would this study of readers in children's books uncover this unease? Would it take us out of the enchanted garden and, if so, where would it lead us?

Another tension that has emerged through the gathering of ideas around fictional children who read has been the interplay of ideas concerning power and empowerment. To claim that reading empowers is unexceptional, and so it is no surprise to find that several authors explore that empowerment. What is surprising is the conclusions they come to. Arizpe (Chapter 5) and Webb (Chapter 7) both consider texts in which young people, for various reasons, struggle to learn to read. One of the questions that these very different explorations of literacy raise is whether reading empowers personally, politically or, in some cases, at all. Liesel eventually learns to read and finds solace and escape in literature. But the street children and rodents in Arizpe's chapter rarely discover that achieving literacy improves their lives: more often, it increases their danger. Like Hanna in *The Reader*, these characters reveal a literary underclass, a section of society for whom reading is shown to be an inappropriate activity. If they transgress by overstepping the rules of society and learning to do it, they are punished.

Reading, then, becomes a matter of politics and gatekeepers are required to control access to text. Both Farrell (Chapter 4) and Smith (Chapter 6) consider issues of access. In Farrell's discussion of magical books in fantasy literature, we see the necessity of the training that is required by young people in many novels before they are granted the privilege of engaging with books of magic. For magic is dangerous: it might open up the possibility of time travel; it might allow the movement between real and fictional worlds; it might imbue in the magician the power to change physical reality, but always, it seems, life is imperilled as a result. The control of literacy in the novels Smith explores is political. What happens to children in societies where text is censored and reading is forbidden? How are their lives and thinking affected by the withdrawal of stories and narratives that might counterpoint and explain the world they know? The chapter shows children who learn to read against the grain of their societies, and who, by doing so, develop political conscience. In the repressive societies in which they live, this too is dangerous. Reading sets them apart as dissidents and activists and puts their lives at risk.

Even in books where reading is not positioned as dangerous and ordinary children are shown reading for interest and relaxation as part of their ordinary lives, we see paradox and change. The way authors in the past and present have used intertextual reference to anchor their stories in their readers' literary thinking has been a matter of interest for a number of scholars. One of the interesting revelations that came from Hunt's work (Chapter 2) was how much writers in the past could take for granted about their readers' range of reference. Arthur Ransome could rely on his readers understanding the references his characters make to the Peaks of Darien, for example. Today, writers can have no such reassurance. The extraordinary proliferation of texts for young people in the last thirty or so years has meant that there can be no reliable canon of children's books that most people can be relied upon to know. What does it mean, we wonder, to be literate in a society where there is so little common textual knowledge?

Some authors writing for young people seem to be asking this question too. In her chapter (Chapter 3) Reynolds looks at a clutch of teen novels that explore reading and romance. In all of them bookish teenagers learn lessons in both. They engage richly and deeply with text, and through that engagement build both individual identity and promising relationships. The authors appear to be showing their characters both what to read and what that reading is good for. Is there a whiff of teacherly purpose here? Are these writers afraid that the texts they value in their own lives and the ways of reading that matter to them will not be available to modern young people unless they are explicitly introduced to them? Jacqueline Wilson seems to think so. Eccleshare (Chapter 8), in her chapter about the changing role of the author, shows how one of the ways that Wilson encourages her myriads of young fans to read beyond her own books is by making characters read the children's classic she loved as a child.

Eccleshare's chapter shows that what children expect from their reading is changing fast. They are knowledgeable about authors and websites and book festivals in a way that was never so before. Those that read, read widely. We wonder, however, if they read deeply. Does the sheer volume of text and meta-text available to children mean that they read *more* texts *more* superficially? Do they have time for the recursive re-reading of favourite texts that took children from less book rich times more and more deeply into story and character? Do they know the books they read less well?

The final three chapters in this volume suggest that though reading has changed, there has been no diminution of engagement. Wolpert and Styles (Chapter 9) and Warnecke (Chapter 10) show the complexity of interaction between reader and text that is needed to make sense of postmodern picturebooks and the sorts of multimodal digital texts that blur the boundaries between novel, film and game. Both chapters stress the activity of the reader: what one has to do or perform to make these texts mean. And it is this performativity that Heath picks up on in the final chapter. She is interested, as always, in the way that words and texts affect what people do. She asks how the books children read help them develop agency, creativity and thoughtfulness. Her answer, like much of the thinking about books and reading in this volume, is ambivalent. There is room for both anxiety and hope.

What this book does not do

There are, of course, many more books about readers and readers in books (and multimodal texts) that might have been mentioned in this volume but are not. One reason for this is that it was not until we started looking that we realised just how many there were – and not just in English.

We make almost no mention of libraries, for instance. There is a rich stream of thinking about libraries in children's literature: they are guardians of knowledge, places of refuge, springboards of opportunity – but we do not explore this. Nor do we say much about reading in school stories. Perhaps the fact that reading seems to occur so rarely so in many of them, or that when it is mentioned it is so often such *functional* reading, is something that deserves study, but we do not present it here. Another gap is contemporary social realism. We say very little here about books about modern children and their reading lives. We know that there is something interesting to be said about Clarice Bean and Ruby Redfort (Child 2011), but we do not say it here. Finally, there is a whole other book to be written about children as writers in children's literature.

The second reason for these omissions is the design of the project. It was our intention that the scholars who participated would be free to choose to work on the texts that interested them at the time, and the texts you see written about here are the ones they chose. We see the enthusiasm they generated for these texts shine through their writing and we think it is a strength of this book: we trust that you will too. And, if any of you feel moved to fill the gaps mentioned above, or to identify others, we will be very pleased for you to do so. There is so much more to say.

An editorial note

In the course of editing this volume a number of decisions had to be made, especially concerning referencing. Dates of publication follow the first mention of all major texts that are mentioned. By 'major' we mean texts that scholars explore in detail or use to substantiate arguments. We do not follow this rule for texts that are merely mentioned or are listed simply as texts read by readers in the stories. We have not provided full references for these 'texts within texts' either. Most are so well known (e.g., *Treasure Island*) that we felt this was unnecessary. Fictional books read by readers in stories are differentiated from real books by having their titles enclose in inverted commas (e.g., "The Emerald Sisters").

Acknowledgments

We would like to thank the British Academy for funding the project *Reading Fictions*. Without them, we would not have been able to run the workshops or the conference at the University of Glasgow that enabled the rich dialogue to take place which culminated in this book. We would like to thank too, the participants: Kim Reynolds, Morag Styles, Maria Nikolajeva, Sylvia Warnecke, Jean Webb, Nikki Gamble, Prue Goodwin, Peter Hunt, Maureen Farrell, Julia Eccleshare and Shirley Brice Heath for their time and their effort and the fun we had together talking about books.

Primary sources

Adams, Douglas. *The Hitchhiker's Guide to the Galaxy*. London: Pan, 1981.
Birkegaard, Mikkel. *The Library of Shadows*. Nunnally, Tina (trans), London: Transworld, 2009.

Calvino, Italo. *On a Winter's Night a Traveller*. Weaver, William (trans), London: Vintage Classics, 1992 [1979].

Child, Lauren. *Ruby Redfort: Look Into My Eyes*. London: Harper Collins Children's Books, 2011.

Docherty, Helen and Docherty, Thomas. *The Snatchabook*. Naperville, IL: Sourcebooks Jabberwocky, 2013.

Eco, Umberto. *The Name of the Rose*. Weaver, William (trans) London: Vintage Classics, 2004 [1980].

Gliori, Debi. *Dragon Loves Penguin*. London: Bloomsbury, 2013.

Gravett, Emily. *Again!* [2011]. London: Simon & Schuster, 2013.

Pamuk, Orhan. *The New Life*. Gun, Guneli (trans), London: Faber and Faber, 2002 [1994].

Ruiz Zafon, Carlos. *The Shadow of the Wind*. Graves, Lucia (trans), London: Orion, 2001.

Schlink, Bernhard. *The Reader*. Brown Janeaway, Carol (trans), London: Vintage. 1995.

Smith, Lane. *It's a Book* [2010]. London: Macmillan Children's Books, 2011.

Zuckerberg, Randi and Berger, Joe. *Dot*. London: HarperCollins, 2013.

Secondary sources

Manguel, Alberto. *The Traveler, the Tower, and the Worm. The Reader as Metaphor*. Philadephia, PA: University of Pensylvania Press, 2013.

Marsh, Jackie. The ghosts of reading past, present and future: The materiality of reading in homes and schools. In K. Hall, U. Goswami, C. Harrison, S. Ellis, and J. Soler (Eds.), *Interdisciplinary Perspectives on Learning to Read: Culture, Cognition and Pedagogy* (pp. 19–31). London: Routledge, 2010.

Pearson, Jaqueline. *Women's Reading in Britain 1750–1834: A Dangerous Recreation*. Cambridge, UK: Cambridge University Press, 1999.

PART I

Reading for life

How do books shape the readers
we become?

1

'EVERYBODY KNEW THAT BOOKS WERE DANGEROUS'

Cognitive and affective responses to representation of books and reading

Maria Nikolajeva

This chapter explores representation of books, literacy, reading and readers through the lens of cognitive literary criticism. This relatively new area of inquiry investigates readers' engagement with fictional texts, including such aspects as understanding of fictionality and literary conventions; extraction of factual, social, ethical and meta-physical knowledge; and not least empathy. Although cognitive literary scholarship is rapidly expanding (see, e.g., Vermeule 2010; Hogan 2011), there is still very little research focused on young readers, whose cognitive and emotional development is different from that of adults (note: different rather than inferior); and on children's and Young Adult literature that ostensibly addresses in a deliberate manner the young audience with this distinct cognitive capacity. Recent scientific experiments that show convincingly that reading fiction enhances theory of mind (e.g., Kidd and Castano 2013) have been conducted with adults.

In the following I consider what kinds of cognitive and emotional responses are evoked by images of books, reading and literacy that we meet in texts targeting a young audience. The inclusion of these representations is obviously intentional, and they have educational as well as aesthetic purpose. Following cognitive criticism, the texts invite readers to engage with the representations, using their life experience, memories and previous literary encounters. The real readers' involvement with the fictional readers' reading affords vicarious pleasure; recognising the concrete books mentioned in the text evokes memories of reading them, hopefully enjoyable memories, but equally memories of grief or fear that reading once may have triggered. In this way readers share with literary characters the experience of having read certain texts. If readers have not read the books relished by characters, the titles may serve as an invitation to read and enjoy them alongside the character. If no concrete titles are mentioned, but characters generally find reading pleasurable, real readers are still expected to engage with this experience cognitively and emotionally; recognising the pleasure that fictional characters find in reading. With the understanding of cognitive and affective engagement with fiction provided by cognitive criticism, this proxy experience is not merely a romantic idea. Through mirror neurons our brains engage with fictional characters' emotions as if they were our own. Reading about reading is just as valuable as reading itself.

The advocates of ethical criticism, particularly Wayne Booth (1988; 2001) and Martha Nussbaum (1995), claim that reading has ethical implications. Nussbaum suggests that readers are given a possibility to act as judges of fictional characters, transferable to real-world situations; she goes as far as to say that reading makes us better people and citizens. While I do not fully share this claim, the educational project of children's literature makes the appearance of books, readers and reading an ethical statement. If we accept the claim that access to literacy and reading is a matter of social justice, then certainly fictional readers can potentially provide excellent role models for real young readers. The problem with employing Nussbaum's ideas of readers as judges is that young readers may not yet have developed the necessary cognitive skills. The positive examples work perfectly if fiction clearly shows that reading has made the fictional character a better person, as Nussbaum would suggest. However, if reading is presented in children's and Young Adult books as having no consequence for the fictional readers or affecting them negatively, as educators and book promoters we are facing a dilemma. We can maintain that the negative representation of reading is a deliberate and ironic device. We can also point out that such representation reflects the view on literacy and reading within a certain historical period and within a particular culture. Children, however, may lack factual knowledge to recognise the socio-historical context, and as they, arguably, are unable to appreciate irony, they can easily miss it. Not least, because the learning brain has difficulty synthesising information provided by different sources and reconciling contradictory statements, young people can simply get confused by the messages they receive from books and from real-life experience. If, as their teachers insist, reading is valuable, why is it so often presented in such an unfavourable light in fiction?

Significant absence

Naturally, to offer readers something to engage with in the first place, there must be representations of books and reading in the texts. Though the present volume offers a wide range of texts featuring books, these texts are not in the majority within children's and Young Adult fiction, classic or modern. One would assume that children's authors might wish to encourage their real readers to read by portraying fictional readers and thus offering the vicarious pleasures of reading suggested above. However, the conspicuous absence of any mention of books, reading or literacy is illuminating. This is true about any genre and mode, and there may be many reasons for such a significant omission. Choosing randomly a number of texts frequently described as classics we hardly find any character with prominent reading habits. What use can Alice make of the poems she knows by heart in a world where all normal rules are cancelled and where words mean whatever someone intends them to mean? The only book featured in the text is boring because it has no pictures or conversations. Why would Jim take a book on his perilous voyage to Treasure Island? What is the value of reading in the land of Oz where the foremost virtues are wit, love and courage? Mary Lennox isn't much of a reader. She receives a gift of books from her uncle, but is only interested in them insofar as they are about gardens and have pictures. Outdoor activities are explicitly presented as healthier and more desirable than poring over books. The Little Prince has no room for books on his tiny planet, and, surprisingly, reading does not feature in the wisdom he gains during his journey. The only reader in the Moomin valley is portrayed as odd: Muskrat who, in the illustrations, is seen to be reading Spengler, which will most likely go unnoticed by young readers. What consolation can reading Aunt Gwen's schoolgirl stories offer to Tom that would prove stronger than his involvement with the midnight garden? Charlie Bucket will not need books in his gastronomic utopia, not even cook books. Lyra who can read signs on her truth machine loses this ability as she learns to read other people's minds instead; yet the text does not suggest that books may provide good guidance for her affective development.

Representation of reading as a pastime does not, of course, provide a good story. Reading is a quiet, lonely occupation, mostly without surprises or conflicts. In adventure stories, both those set in alternative worlds and in quasi-realistic environments, the characters are too busy saving the world, exposing criminals or finding treasures. These activities may involve reading a secret message, so literacy is occasionally presented as an asset, but reading as a pastime is too slow and peaceful to fit into adventure plots, and preparing for adventures, few characters pack books to keep them company, although they may occasionally need a book or a map for guidance in their quest. Not even in many school stories, where books might be expected to be prominent, is reading in any way presented as pleasurable. If anything, reading in school is boring and joyless. Yet many adventure and school-stories characters who we do not remember as passionate readers do in fact read for pleasure, including William and the Famous Five.

In dystopias, children and young people are frequently illiterate, as literacy is a threat to the depicted establishment. The totalitarian regimes featured in dystopias know very well how to manipulate their subjects through denying them literacy or banning books. In Frances Hardinge's *Fly by Night* (2011 [2005]), books are viewed as dangerous by authorities, and rumours are deliberately spread to discourage people from reading. During the 'bad times', books are burned, and people who possessed books were prosecuted and killed. From the point of view of reader engagement, this representation of books and literacy is ambivalent. An expert reader is expected to see through the narrator's irony as well as the character's ignorance. The free indirect discourse employed in the recurrent statements such as 'Everybody knew that books were dangerous' reflects the main character's understanding of the situation, and her attitude is confirmed by the fact that her father was indeed prosecuted for his writing. Mosca has been brought up to love words, including complicated words that she does not understand; she savours words as spices. Reading has equipped her with knowledge that helps her survive (see Smith, this volume).

In contrast, Katniss in Suzanne Collins's *The Hunger Games* (2008) has no use for literacy in her struggle for survival. (Ironically, if Katniss and her creator had read some cognitive criticism they would know that reading is essential for survival.) As readers we have privilege over Katniss because we know that, based on genre conventions, she will win the games. This metacritical knowledge is easy to miss in our assessment of reader engagement. On the other hand, the characters' as well as the readers' genre expectation prove hardly helpful in China Mieville's *Un Lun Dun* (2008 [2007]), while the characters' literacy is of little use. Even the animated, sentient book of the novel admits its own uselessness.

In contemporary Young Adult novels, the protagonists are too preoccupied with their personal concerns and relationships to have spare time for reading. Although some adolescent characters find support and consolation in reading and writing, they are in the minority. A typical adolescent character, boy and girl alike, is a non-reader. They may be consumers of other kinds of texts, including films, comics, song lyrics, blogs and twitter; yet they seldom read what is habitually called quality fiction. Moreover, they find classroom-assigned reading tedious. Paradoxically, and not particularly credibly, these non-readers are frequently skilful writers: diary writers, letter writers, memoir writers, confessions writers – one may wonder where their eloquence comes from if they have never read a book. Naturally, this is a legitimate poetic licence; yet I much prefer the gradual change of the narrator in *Dear Mr. Henshaw* (1983), by Beverly Cleary, whose amazing linguistic and existential development is inspired by his favourite author.

Characters who are allegedly high-performers in school are not necessarily readers. Dante, the protagonist of Malorie Blackman's *Boys Don't Cry* (2010), who receives four A-stars for his A levels, is not shown reading anything except anonymous picturebooks, which are presented as pacifiers to make his baby go to sleep rather than an enjoyment shared by parent and child. True, Dante is far too busy with the unexpected burden of single teenage fatherhood, as well as his younger brother's coming out, to have time or energy to read. If Dante had been narratively constructed as a mathematical genius or a computer nerd, the absence of books in his life might be explicable. However, Dante intends to go to university to study history; he envisions a career in humanities, possibly journalism; he says he wants to investigate the truth. In other words, I find it implausible that a character like Dante is not surrounded by books. At the very least, he might be likely to use the lonely hours when his baby daughter takes her naps to find solace in a book. When Dante's father buys books for the baby, the plot offers an excellent opportunity for the character/narrator to express the joy of recognition in encountering his own childhood favourites that he will now be able to share with his daughter. Yet reading is intentionally omitted from the wide palette of characterisation devices, which I cannot but view as an artistic flaw.

Going further through genres and kinds of children's and Young Adult fiction, animal stories do not feature books unless the characters are fully anthropomorphic and not necessarily then either. In picturebooks for very young readers, whether they have human or anthropomorphic characters, reading may simply be irrelevant as picturebooks tend to focus on a particular and limited episode in which reading has no function. (There are, of course, scores of picturebooks featuring books and reading, which is a topic in itself, see Wolpert and Styles, this volume.)

One may argue that the abundance of non-readers in children's fiction is of little consequence because the characters engage in a range of other activities that present various facets of their identity: adventures, sports, social life, emergent sexuality, parental conflicts. Yet once again, what kind of messages about the value of reading does the significant absence convey? Cognitive criticism pays strong attention to the issue of empathy, the ability to understand other people's states of mind (see Zunshine 2006; Keen 2008). Engaging affectively with literary characters, we are able to penetrate their minds in a way impossible in real life. There is, however, a risk of young readers engaging too strongly, which is often referred to as identification, or more precisely immersive identification. This is a rather immature readerly position as it implies aligning with the character and thus being unable to assess their state of mind as separate from one's own. In case of fictional non-readers, engaging with them immersively, we uncritically accept that, for the character, and by extension for ourselves, reading is of no value because there are other, more important things to do. Empathy, on the other hand, that does not presuppose sharing the character's feelings, views, beliefs, opinions or assumptions, allows us to state that, though reading does not seem to be valuable for the character, we still see the value of it for ourselves, at the very least, non-reading being different from our own experience. Empathy, as cognitive science points out, does not develop until late adolescence, so most young readers are likely to identify with fictional non-readers immersively.

We do not normally register the absence of an element in a text unless it is brought to our attention. Yet the consistent absence of an element in fictional texts that these very texts represent is an ambivalent message, and it becomes still more ambivalent when we consider some texts that do feature books and reading, implicitly or explicitly.

Implicit readers

There are texts that do not show children actually reading, but make it obvious that they are somehow familiar with stories and act them out in their games. We would probably not associate Tom Sawyer with extensive reading, but he has apparently got inspiration for his Robin Hood and other performances from chapbooks, and he and Becky must be familiar with romance conventions. Shirley, in John Burningham's picturebooks, clearly finds inspiration for her imaginary adventures from books about pirates and knights.

There are, however, texts in which books are implicitly harmful. No books are mentioned by title in *Anne of Green Gables* (1908), yet there is no doubt that Anne has got her foolish romantic ideas and high-flown language from books. As she eventually learns to overcome her mode of thinking and talking, it is to be assumed that reading has had a negative effect on her, the consequences of which must be eliminated. In Anne's case, this implication is particularly self-contradictory, because education is presented as an important part of Anne's personal development. Such negative view of books and reading is prominent in classic mainstream novels in which young ladies who read books, especially 'French novels', are warned that they will never get married. This is a highly ambivalent message, as at the same time a young lady is supposed to be well educated to find a good match. Apparently, novel reading does not constitute a part of proper education. In engaging with Anne, we are met with a set of clashing statements. Anne is a lovable character, not least because of her wild imagination. Though there is no reason for us to question it, the narrator prompts us to infer that imagination stimulated by excessive reading is undesirable. As cognitive criticism points out, young brains may have difficulties reconciling contradictory information. The view on reading in *Anne of Green Gables* can be highly confusing.

A character such as Pippi Longstocking explicitly conveys that reading is of little use. Not only are books conspicuously absent from Pippi's abundant possessions, but her whole attitude shows that a child can have a happy and harmonious existence without education. Somehow, Pippi knows everything she needs to know, from the capital of Portugal to baking gingerbread, but apparently she has not acquired her knowledge from books. She turns a school inspection into a farce; and when she needs to write a party invitation she is not bothered about correct spelling.

This brings in the question of authorial intention. I admit that Mark Twain intended Tom's inspiration from books to be a parody. I also admit that Burnett makes a case for a healthy lifestyle, and that Montgomery shows that too wild imagination is incompatible with the scope of freedom a modern young woman can aspire to achieve. However, I suspect that Astrid Lindgren has a more subtle project than just questioning literacy as a virtue. She questions school as authority and learning as power exercise, and she celebrates the competent child who can decide herself when and how she wants to be educated. Obviously, in practicalities of life, Pippi is better equipped than her literate playmates. And yet what kind of attitude toward literacy will readers find in the Pippi books? Will they recognise themselves as readers or will they put the book aside and go and stage a shipwreck instead? This is a question of empathy that cognitive criticism has focused on. As mature readers, we should be able to empathise with characters who do not express or share our values. We should be able to understand Tom's or Anne's or Pippi's emotions even though we do not judge them to be passionate readers. We need to realise and admit that we are enjoying the characters' adventures, joys and sorrows vicariously, through reading, and that without reading we would be deprived of the enjoyment. To put it in a highly oversimplified manner, we should feel sorry for the poor fictitious children who have no access to the wide world of fiction. However, such an approach needs a good deal of sophistication, and I suspect that young readers' natural response would be observing that the most exciting fictional characters don't read books. At best, they might be aware of genre conventions, such as robins being benevolent (Narnia) and heroes inevitably getting rescued (Moomin books).

The social harm of literacy

Attitude toward and engagement with reading and literacy as a characterisation device is a fascinating issue, arguably more pertinent to children's literature than the mainstream. This negative portrayal of reading permeates contemporary children's and Young Adult fiction in which loners, outsiders, newcomers, underperformers, overweighters, eyeglass-wearers are all avid readers, as opposed to popular, successful, physically attractive, but frequently light-headed and shallow pseudo-heroes. Symptomatically, gender differences are negligible. In real-life surveys, girls of all age groups seem to read more than boys. In fictional representations of reading, stereo-typical readers and non-readers are equally often girls and boys. The message is disturbingly ambiguous. The underdog typically wins over the false superstar, not least through the knowledge and experience gained from books. Yet the new identity that includes social status, academic or athletic achievements, inevitably implies the loss of the joy of reading and even the necessary time to read. It seems that you cannot eat the cake and have it. For popularity among peers, reading must be sacrificed. Consider Bella in *Twilight* (2005). When she is a newcomer and an outsider, she finds some consolation in books. Moreover, at least one book mentioned by title, *Wuthering Heights*, provides ample characterisation through reading preferences. However, Bella quickly becomes far too busy to have time to read. Possibly, if she had read *Dracula*, she would have been better prepared for dealing with vampires. This example adheres to the pattern I have already outlined. Although reading provides some consolation to a newcomer and social outcast, as soon as the character gains in social position, they inevitably abandon their dedication to books.

If actual readers initially empathise with the underdog – which would be natural as they are readers themselves – the development leads to the same conclusion I have suggested for the presumptive reader of *Pippi*. Because reading endangers social position it must be avoided. Will real young readers be mature enough to disengage themselves from the imposed subjectivity of the text and realise that, although the protagonist gives up reading for the sake of social status, this is in fact not the right strategy?

Interestingly, this aspect echoes the idea of literacy as lost innocence that appears in many classic children's books. In *Heidi* (1881), for instance, learning to read is clearly presented as an inevitable loss of the protagonist's natural state and her entry into civilisation, which she subsequently imposes on others (see Nikolajeva 2000). Likewise, Christopher Robin's final mastery of spelling leads to his expulsion from the paradise of childhood (see Nikolajeva 2010, pp. 27–40). The lonely readers of contemporary realist novels have presumably learned to read and lost their connection with nature and with other people; lost themselves in fiction.

Yet, even when reading is superficially presented as beneficial, on closer consideration it is highly ambiguous. Caitlin, the narrator and character of Kathryn Erskine's *Mockingbird* (2012 [2010], p. 41), boasts of being an experienced and fast reader.

> I find thirty-two books in the library … . Dad talks with the librarian and says it's okay for me to use his card too so that I can check out a lot of books.

> Some of them are kids' books and some are adult books but I can read any-thing because my reading score is so high they can't even rate it.

There are no books mentioned by title in the text, while the narrative in which Caitlin finds a role model for herself, her brother and her father, *To Kill a Mockingbird*, is the film adaptation, not the novel, which in a way questions the value of reading. Caitlin seems to be one of those supertalented children who have the technical skills of reading, but who do not really get engrossed in books. In fact, because Caitlin, an Asperger's sufferer, lacks empathy, she hardly engages with fiction at all, and the text misses the opportunity to show how reading fiction might assist Caitlin in under-standing other people's emotions. On the contrary, the narrator points out that she enjoys reading exactly because books are predictable and do not force her to employ empathy:

> What's great about books is that the stuff inside doesn't change. People say you can't judge the book by the cover but that's not true because it says right on the cover what's inside. And no matter how many times you read the book the words and pictures don't change … . Books are not like people. Books are safe.
>
> *(p. 42)*

Ostensibly, the text expects the reader to understand that Caitlin's attitude toward books and reading is immature; that is, to evaluate her unreliability as a narrator. However, even for readers without any social disability, the discrepancy between the young narrator's statement and the message that the text wants to convey may be difficult to perceive. Thus, Caitlin's escape from the real world where she lacks social skills to fictional worlds in which she does not have to employ social skills seems harmful rather than liberating, which real readers may assess in an undesirable way. Moreover, as we are not given any indication of the scope of Caitlin's reading, we can infer either that she reads only simplistic books that do not encourage empathy (which is unlikely as she presents herself as omnivorous in her reading) or that she reads superficially, not engaging with empathy, just as she does with real people.

The emotional harm of reading

Still more alarming are books that present books as causing emotional instability. The female protagonist of Anthony Browne's picturebook *The Tunnel* (1989) falls victim of fears evoked by reading. Not surprisingly, she reads fairy tales, which have by many educators, from Rousseau to the present day, been viewed as unsuitable and harmful for young readers. We may argue that the final reconciliation of the fairy-tale book and the ball on the back endpapers, noted by many scholars, can be equally interpreted as the book's (that is, sister's) submission to the ball (brother); once again, the priority of the healthy outdoor activities over the unhealthy indoor fiction perusal.

Peter Pan (1911) shows clearly the power of stories and storytelling, if not of printed books. Yet it also shows the risks of entering stories and the danger of getting stuck in stories. Wendy chooses to return to the real world, whereas Peter prefers to stay forever the immortalised protagonist of his own story. This danger of reading as escape is perhaps nowhere as prominent as in Michael Ende's *The Neverending Story* (1984 [1979]), in which the fictional reader eventually breaches the boundary between his own fictional world and the hypofiction of the book in the book. The price is high, and it takes the protagonist a long time to find his way back home, which suggests that losing yourself in fiction may not provide a solution of real problems. It can be argued that Bastian returns home with new experience that will enable him to cope with problems; yet for some reason the author chooses a book rather than a wardrobe as a portal to the alternative world. (Bastian is, incidentally, a book thief, which may or may not be relevant to the title of a later novel.) Again, with my slightly provocative scepticism, I may ask whether the message to the reader is: don't get too involved with the story, you may get stuck (or, if we prefer, addicted). In fact, this is a cognitive and empathic issue. Firstly, mature readers are expected to distinguish between fact and fiction. Famously, we employ suspension of disbelief when we read; yet if suspension goes over to permanent enchantment, we have lost control, like the Knight of the Sorrowful Countenance. Secondly, by identifying entirely with the fiction we are reading, we lose our own identity and subjectivity, which is exactly what happens to Bastian in *The Neverending Story*. The novel portrays a reader who learns to overcome the seductive power of fiction; in fact, a reader who goes over from identification to empathy, from solipsistic self-pity to understanding other people's concerns. The question is, however, whether an average young reader of the novel is capable of this second-order empathy.

Far Rockaway (2013 [2011]), by Charlie Fletcher, echoes *The Neverending Story* in its device of placing the character within fictional narratives. The reason given in the text is, however, radically different. The protagonist, Cat, is in a coma after a traffic accident. In her comatose dreams, or rather nightmares, she enters the numerous fictional worlds from novels that her grandfather has read with her. I assume that the author intends the metanarratives to be recognised by the reader, although few are part of the average young audience's experience today. Even if readers are not familiar with every text alluded to, it is clear that all the characters and settings come from Cat's reading. Yet the device of mixing together characters from different fictional stories is dubious since it suggests that literary characters have a life outside their story. The transparent metaphor of the novel is that getting immersed in fiction is equal to dying, the idea implicit in *Peter Pan* as well as *The Neverending Story*. This is a highly ambiguous proposition. Cat finds herself in fictions that her grandfather has introduced her to, and she also meets him in the metafictional narratives. Living inside fiction has no healing effect, rather the other way round. The solution is that Cat should leave the world of fiction – and by implication, the memories of her grandfather – behind and return to real life. Once again, reading appears socially and emotionally harmful, because it cannot be shared by the protagonist's surroundings.

She has to be rescued from it, and she is brought back from enchantment by her brother's music.

The proxy experience

I would not wish to end this chapter on such a pessimistic note. As demonstrated in the other chapters, there are scores of texts that present books as a source of knowledge and joy, and literacy and reading as valuable. In numerous fantasy novels magical books prove instrumental for characters' goals (see Farrell's chapter, this volume). This includes the *Harry Potter* novels – and I believe we don't think of Harry as an avid reader. My focus is, however, the cognitive and emotional investment that readers are expected to make in the fictional characters who engage in reading – or do not engage in reading.

Such vicarious learning is perhaps more important than the images of books and reading as such. What do fictional readers learn from books? Tom Sawyer and Anne Shirley have acquired a false picture of reality from the books they have read, and the March sisters pattern their life journeys after the symbolical journey in *Pilgrim's Progress*. The enumeration of books that Jerusha Abbott in *Daddy-Long-Legs* (1912) realises she has not read is a good initial reading list for any beginning reader. Leslie in *Bridge to Terabithia* (1977) has managed to extract spiritual wisdom from *Hamlet*, *Moby-Dick* and the Narnia Chronicles and to share it with Jess. Books that the young protagonist in Guus Kuijer's *The Book of Everything* (2004) borrows from his neighbour, an old lady with the reputation of a witch, give him strength to oppose his tyrannical father. In *Forbidden* (2010), by Tabitha Suzuma, *Romeo and Juliet* contributes to emphasising the image scheme of star-crossed lovers, while *Hamlet* brings in the issue of incest. The protagonist's familiarity with *Midsummer Night's Dream* in Susan Cooper's *King of Shadows* (1999) helps him cope with his inexplicable time displacement to Shakespeare's London. Rosalind in Jacqueline Wilson's *Four Children and It* (2012) demonstrates the advantage of being well-read when dealing with magic in the twenty-first century.

There are scores of books in which other real books are mentioned or alluded to – some discussed in other chapters of this volume. Some intentions behind such inclusions can be that authors are trying to legitimise their own position ('I am in good company'), or guide the readers ('That's the way you should understand my story – it is based on …'), or invite readers to share their own superiority ('Have you read and recognised all titles mentioned?'). Sometimes a text mentions 'the assistant pigkeeper', and if readers get the allusion, so much the better, and if not, they still know it must be a book, and if encountered later, it will give them aesthetic pleasure.

Obviously, lots of fictional characters gain factual knowledge, as well as knowledge of social norms, beliefs, ethics, from books, and thus share this knowledge with actual readers. Such embedded knowledge may be more valuable when obtained through empathy with a literary character than directly from a didactic narrator.

Yet there are also lessons to be learned from fictional characters' emotional engagement with fiction. In John Green's *The Fault in Our Stars* (2012), Hazel is an avid reader, but there is one specific book that provides her with spiritual guidance. It is a fictional book written by a fictional author, and it is used to reflect Hazel's own life situation. In this metanovel, Hazel, a terminal cancer patient, hopes to find answers to questions that life cannot provide her with. Hazel is an immersive reader; she fully identifies with the protagonist of the novel; moreover, she perceives fictional characters as if they were real people who have an existence outside the narrative. Hazel does understand that the interrupted first-person narrative most probably indicates that the character/narrator is dead; yet she compulsively needs to find out what has happened to the other characters. As a reader, Hazel employs life-to-text strategy, projecting her own experience into the fictional narrative. With her reason, she has accepted her own imminent death, mirrored by the death of the metanovel character, yet emotionally she seems unable to reconcile with the idea that there is nothing after death, that is, employ the text-to-life wisdom and view death as a definite interruption. Hazel approaches the metafictional author to seek answers to her questions and is bitterly disappointed when the author dismisses her.

As readers, we are asked to perform a number of cognitive operations. Firstly, we must detach ourselves from Hazel's subject position. As her story is so poignant and engaging, we wish to 'become' Hazel, to share her experience. On the other hand, few of us have fortunately been through anything near Hazel's experience of terminal cancer at the age of sixteen, which means that we need to employ empathy, but not necessarily get under her skin. In respect to Hazel's involvement with the metanovel, we are expected to understand that Hazel's pursuit is futile. Even if the cynical fictional author provides a further life for the secondary characters, the main character's fate would not be affected by it. The purpose of the metanovel is, apart from providing the engine for the plot, to guide us as readers toward a more mature reading. For instance, we are not supposed to expect a sequel after the text is concluded. We are urged to understand that authors are not omniscient and omnipotent gods who can offer answers to all questions, but that the meaning of a text is revealed through the interaction with a reader and can differ from reader to reader. Although we never learn anything substantial about the metanovel beyond the elementary plot, a set of characters and a handful of pseudo-philosophical quotations, it is used as an example of what reading can do and how the absence of ready-made answers forces Hazel to think for herself. Although reading as such cannot be viewed as the central theme of *The Fault in Our Stars*, in the same manner as it is, for instance, in *The Neverending Story*, the value and positive effect of fiction is emphasised in that Hazel comes to a better understanding of herself through learning to empathise with a fictional character without immersive identification (for a more romantic perspective on this novel, see Reynolds' chapter in this section).

Another metabook that provides guidance is featured in Marcus Sedgwick's *She Is Not Invisible* (2013). The protagonist/narrator, sixteen-year-old Laureth, is blind, which does not prevent her from being a passionate consumer of fiction. Still, her disability proves a major disadvantage when she is confronted with hand-written text, not easily transferrable to audiotext by her clever technical aid. In her quest, she is not only dependent on her little brother for practical purposes, such as leading her around, but also on his literacy. Laureth's father is a writer – a relatively common figure in children's and Young Adult fiction, ostensibly autobiographical or at least metafictional. After a successful career of 'funny books' he decides to write something serious, something that reveals truth, whereby he not only loses his audience and income, but is also about to lose his family. The book never gets written, and Laureth only partakes of her father's scribbled notes that give her clues about his mysterious disappearance. On one level the novel is a quick-paced adventure just on the edge of the implausible, almost a tall-tale. It is not a 'disability book', echoing Hazel's statement in *The Fault in Our Stars* that 'cancer books suck' (p. 48). Yet its main thrust is the protagonist's self-knowledge through an unwritten book, a paradox that chimes perfectly with her impairment.

I do not feel I can draw any conclusions from the argument above. Yet there is another, perhaps unexpected concern for us to consider. If we know little about how young readers engage with fiction in conventional, printed form, we know nothing whatsoever about their cognitive and emotional engagement with digital books. We do not know whether digital media stimulate our empathy differently from printed media. As digital reading devices take over printed books in the real world they will inevitably invade the fictional world of children's and Young Adult literature. How will future readers, grown up with electronic devices, engage with fictional readers of printed books?

Primary sources

Alcott, Louisa May. *Little Women* [1868]. Harmondsworth: Penguin, 1994.

Barrie, James M. *Peter Pan and Wendy* [1911]. In *Peter Pan in Kensington Gardens / Peter and Wendy*. Oxford: Oxford University Press, 2012.

Baum, L. Frank. *The Wonderful Wizard of Oz* [1900]. New York: HarperCollins, 2000.

Blackman, Malorie. *Boys Don't Cry*. London: Doubleday, 2010.

Blyton, Enid. *Five on a Treasure Island*. London: Hodder and Stoughton, 1942.

Browne, Anthony. *The Tunnel*. London: Julia McRae, 1989.

Burnett, Frances Hodgson. *The Secret Garden* [1911]. London: Penguin, 1995.

Burningham, John. *Come Away From the Water, Shirley*. New York: Crowell, 1977.

Carroll, Lewis. *Alice's Adventures in Wonderland* [1865]. Oxford: Oxford University Press, 2009.

Cleary, Beverly. *Dear Mr. Henshaw*. New York: Morrow, 1983.

Collins, Suzanne. *The Hunger Games*. New York: Scholastic, 2008.

Cooper, Susan. *King of Shadows*. London: The Bodley Head, 1999.

Crompton, Richmal. *Just William*. London: Newness, 1922.

Dahl, Roald. *Charlie and the Chocolate Factory* [1964]. London: Puffin, 2013.

Ende, Michael. *The Neverending Story* [1979]. New York: Penguin, 1984.

Erskine, Kathryn. *Mockingbird* [2010]. New York: Usborne, 2012.

Fletcher, Charlie. *Far Rockaway* [2011]. London: Hodder, 2013.

Green, John. *The Fault in Our Stars*. New York: Penguin, 2012.

Hardinge, Frances. *Fly by Night* [2005]. London: Macmillan, 2011.

Jansson, Tove. *Finn Family Moomintroll* [1948]. London: Benn, 1950.

Kuijer, Guus. *The Book of Everything* [2004]. London: Arthur A. Levine, English edition 2006.

Lewis, C. S. *The Lion, the Witch and the Wardrobe*. London: The Bodley Head, 1950.

Lindgren, Astrid. *Pippi Longstocking* [1945]. Oxford: Oxford University Press, 2007.

Meyer, Stephenie. *Twilight*. London: Atom, 2005.

Mieville, China. *Un Lun Dun* [2007]. London: Macmillan, 2008.

Milne, A. A. *The House At Pooh Corner*. London: Methuen, 1928.

Montgomery, L. M. *Anne of Green Gables* [1908]. New York: Bantam, 1992.

Paterson, Katherine. *Bridge to Terabithia*. New York: HarperCollins, 1977.

Pearce, Philippa. *Tom's Midnight Garden*. Oxford: Oxford University Press, 1958.

Pullman, Philip. *Northern Lights*. London: Scholastic, 1995.

Rowling, J. K. *Harry Potter and the Philosopher's Stone*. London: Bloomsbury, 1997.

Saint-Exupéry, Antoine de. *The Little Prince* [1943]. Harmonsworth: Penguin, 1962.

Sedgwick, Marcus. *She is Not Invisible*. London: Indigo, 2013.

Spyri, Johanna. *Heidi* [1881]. London: Wordsworth, 1993.

Stevenson, Robert Louis. *Treasure Island* [1883]. London: Penguin, 2008.

Suzuma, Tabitha. *Forbidden*. London: Random House, 2010.

Twain, Mark. *The Adventures of Tom Sawyer* [1876]. Harmondsworth, Penguin, 1985.

Webster, Jean. *Daddy-Long-Legs* [1912]. Harmondsworth: Penguin, 1995.

Wilson, Jacqueline. *Four Children and It*. London: Puffin, 2012.

Secondary sources

Booth, Wayne C. *The Company We Keep: An Ethics of Fiction*. Berkeley, CA: University of California Press, 1988. Print.

Booth, Wayne C. "Why Ethical Criticism Can Never Be Simple". In Todd F. Davis and Kenneth Womack (Eds.), *Mapping the Ethical Turn: A Reader in Ethics, Culture, and Literary Theory* (pp. 16–29). Charlottesville, VA: University Press of Virginia, 2001. Print.

Hogan, Patrick Colm. *What Literature Teaches Us about Emotions*. Cambridge: Cambridge University Press, 2011. Print.

Keen, Suzanne. *Empathy and the Novel*. Oxford: Oxford University Press, 2008. Print.

Kidd, D. C. and Castano, E. Reading literary fiction improves theory of mind. *Science*, October 3, 2013. DOI: 10.1126/science.1239918. Online.

Nikolajeva, Maria. Tamed imagination. A rereading of Heidi. *Children's Literature Association Quarterly*, 2, 68–75. 2000. Print.

Nikolajeva, Maria. *Power, Voice and Subjectivity in Literature for Young Readers*. New York: Routledge, 2010. Print.

Nussbaum, Martha C. *Poetic Justice: The Literary Imagination and Public Life*. Boston, MA: Beacon Press, 1995. Print.

Vermeule, Blakey. *Why Do We Care about Literary Characters?* Baltimore, MD: Johns Hopkins University Press, 2010. Print.

Zunshine, Lisa. *Why We Read Fiction: Theory of Mind and the Novel*. Columbus, OH: The Ohio State University Press, 2006. Print.

2

TAKEN AS READ

Readers in books and the importance of reading, 1744–2003

Peter Hunt

The depiction of fictional child readers reading books in books of fiction for child readers raises fascinating questions of how far this endorses reading, and how far the nature of the endorsement shifts with time and cultural change. From John Newbery in the eighteenth century, to *The League of Extraordinary Gentlemen* in the twenty-first century, printed fiction references printed fiction, often through the image of the child protagonist reading, or what the child protagonist has read. That this has persisted despite the shift to 'new' media suggests (in the writers) a positive endorsement of a particular kind of ('book') literacy, whereas in the past it might better be seen as a confirmation of the processes of a natural reading community.

This chapter considers the strength of a particular tradition of intertextual reference, from Richard Jefferies, through Arthur Ransome to Aidan Chambers and Terry Pratchett. This is the 'mainstream' British children's literature canon, and it consists of books that may be canonical precisely because they feature books and book-readers, and thus support a particular attitude to and valuation of reading and literacy.

From the beginning of commercial children's books in Britain with John Newbery in the 1740s, until the 1990s, books (and reading) were the natural intertextual and intra-textual references in and drivers of fiction. It was natural to name books in books; it was natural to show characters reading books and being influenced by books; it was an acknowledgement that book-reading was a normal part of the lives of the readers and the characters they read about; and it was an acknowledgement of shared attitudes and shared knowledge.

If one subscribes to Aidan Chambers's view of book-reading, which most writers of this extended period clearly did, then there existed a symbiotic virtuous circle.

> Because book-writing, by which I mean literary writing, is the best means by which we express what is innermost, and because book-reading leaves the

entire act of interpretation to the reader's inner self, we not only become intimately closer to the consciousness of another person than is possible in any other way but are also engaged in our own consciousness more intricately and more actively than by any other means. This is why we so often feel when we have read a great book, a book that matters to us, that we have grown, that we are more aware of some aspect of ourself, of other people, of life itself, than we were before... To put it like this is, of course, to make a religious statement.

(Chambers 2001, p. 27)

Which, of course, it is – and it is not surprising that Chambers's own novels, especially *Breaktime* (1978) are suffused with references to books: *Breaktime* is a metafiction about the relationship between books and reality – its hero, 'Ditto', is referred to by his lover as 'word child'. Chambers's, *Dying to Know You* (2012) centres on reading. But is Chambers the last of his line? His friend Alan Garner's *The Stone Book Quartet* (1976), which is about generational politics of reading and power, seems to renounce reading in favour of intuition. At the end of the first novella, Mary's stonemason father gives her a book fashioned from stone: the dead end of reading:

He gave Mary a prayer book bound in blue-black calf skin, tooled, stitched and decorated. It was only by the weight that she could tell it was stone and not leather.

'It's better than a book you can open,' said Father. 'A book has only one story ...'

Mary turned the stone over. Father had split it so that the back showed two fronds of a plant, like the silk in skeins, like the silk on the water under the hill ...

And Mary sat by the fire and read the stone book that had in it all the stories of the world and the flowers of the flood.

(Garner 1976, pp. 49–51)

Certainly in the 1970s and 1980s (as today) it seemed to many working in education and with children's books as though literacy itself was at stake: critics and educators such as Margaret Meek and Geoff Fox published some of their most powerful and evangelical work in support of reading (e.g., Meek 1988 and Benton and Fox 1985). In 1988 the neo-conservative Roald Dahl (see Sturrock 2010) weighed in with his now notorious reading-list in *Matilda* which included some raw (and unedited) propagandising for the more heavyweight classics.

Over the next few afternoons Mrs Phelps could hardly take her eyes from the small girl sitting for hour after hour in the big armchair at the far end of the room with the book on her lap. It was necessary to rest it on the lap because it was too heavy for her to hold up, which meant she had to sit leaning forward in order to read. And a strange sight it was, this tiny dark-haired person ... totally absorbed ... by the spell of magic that Dickens the great story-teller had woven with his words.

(Dahl 1989 [1988], pp. 15–16)

The first part of the book contrasts Matilda's virtuously voracious reading with the uncivilised, not to say barbaric, TV-watching non-readers of her family. (This, of course, follows the 99-line rant by the Oompa-Loompas in *Charlie and the Chocolate Factory* (1964) – 'Go throw your TV set away / And in its place you can install / A lovely bookshelf on the wall ...' (Dahl 2001 [1964], pp. 174–175).) It seems that this strident validation of books and reading was a sign that the reading of books needed to be championed, even for readers who were already reading a book. How far had the habit of reading declined, and how far does its appearance in fictional texts reflect the situation of reading *outside* the texts?

On the face of it, it is rather surprising that books show people reading at all; with the exception of metafictions, book-reading is not very interesting to *watch*, and there is an inherent paradox in readers escaping into a book to watch characters escaping *from* books through books. Early British children's books featured children reading as part of the evangelical/educational message – as in Mary Louisa Charlesworth's *Ministering Children* (1854), whereas in the twentieth century, fictional characters who read are often seen as inferior, deviant beings – nerds. However, there is a long and positive tradition of finding child readers *in* books, despite the marginalising of education and reading in fiction from Lewis Carroll onwards. Alice's famous rejection of books – '... once or twice she had peeped into the book her sister was reading, but it had no pictures or conversations in it, "and what is the use of a book," thought Alice, "without pictures or conversations"'— and the merciless parodies of school-lesson verses that follow led to one of Carroll's unlikely legacies. School work – reading, education – became irrelevant to holiday adventures, or merely a source of comedy (as with the school stories of Frank Richards, Anthony Buckeridge and hundreds of others).

However, the central tradition of British children's books took fiction as its starting point, characters often leading a double life of reality and book-fuelled fantasy. Richard Jefferies's *Bevis, the Story of a Boy* (1882) – which, although initially published as a three-decker novel, was soon adopted by, and adapted for children (by no less than G. A. Henty) – can be taken as marking the beginning of this tradition. *Bevis* is thoroughly 'action-based' but, between sailing and building huts and making a gun and shooting things, Bevis takes a break:

When they got home he put his books together – the 'Odyssey', Don Quixote, the grey and battered volume of ballads [*Percy's Reliques*] a tiny little book of Shakespeare's poems, of which he had lately become very fond, and Filmore's rhymed translation of Faust.

(Jefferies 1989 [1882], p. 236)

There is plenty of reference by implication to empire-building stories and sea stories:

> 'We ought not to fight now,' said Bevis. 'You know we are exploring; people never fight then, else the savages kill those who are left; they wait till they get home, and then fight.'
>
> *(pp. 53–54)*

> 'The proper thing is, to shoot you under the table,' said Bevis. 'That's what buccaneers do.'
>
> *(p. 261)*

Jefferies (himself a bookish outdoors-man) points up one of the basic paradoxes:

> 'What you really want to know is never in a book, and no-one can tell you. By-and-by, if you keep it steadily in memory and ever have your eyes open, you hit on it by accident.'
>
> *(p. 193)*

But, generally, in the late nineteenth century and early twentieth century, books were approved of in books. In *Little Women* (1868) Jo March is introduced on the first page as 'a bookworm' who wants to buy Friedrich de la Motte Fouqué's *Undine and Sintram*; and in Chapter 11, famously, 'Jo spent the morning on the river with Laurie, and the afternoon reading and crying over *The Wide, Wide World*, up in the apple tree' (Alcott 1953 [1868], pp. 12, 145.) In Frances Hodgson Burnett's *Little Lord Fauntleroy* (1886), Cedric Errol's English nursery has 'shelves full of books' (Hodgson Burnett 1993 [1886], p. 78), and Captain Crewe in Burnett's *A Little Princess* (1905) has no (real) problem with them and his daughter Sara (who is seven):

> 'I am not in the least anxious about her education,' Captain Crewe said, with his gay laugh, as he held Sara's hand and patted it. 'The difficulty will be to keep her from learning too fast and too much. She is always sitting with her little nose burrowing into books. She doesn't read them, Miss Minchin; she gobbles them up as if she were a little wolf instead of a little girl. She is always starving for new books to gobble, and she wants grown-up books – great, big, fat ones – French and German as well as English – history and geography and poets, and all sorts of things. Drag her away from her books when she reads too much. Make her ride her pony in the Row or go out and buy a new doll ...'.
>
> *(Hodgson Burnett 2002 [1905], pp. 9–10)*

And even if Mary Lennox doesn't have much time for fairy tales in Burnett's *The Secret Garden* (1911), and Mrs Medlock's account of Misselthwaite Manor 'sounded like something in a book and ... did not make Mary feel cheerful' (Hodgson Burnett 2011 [1911], p. 15) nevertheless, Colin's library, at first tiresome, grows with the children to be an empowering element.

Elsewhere, there are plenty of references to children reading, and to what they have read. E. Nesbit's *The Story of the Treasure Seekers* (1899) begins with a reflection on reading from Oswald, the child narrator:

> I have often thought that if the people who write books for children knew a little more it would be better. I shall not tell you anything about us except what I should like to know about if I was reading the story and you were writing it. Albert's uncle says I should have put this in the preface, but I never read prefaces and it is not much good writing things just for people to skip. I wonder other authors have never thought of this.
>
> *(Nesbit 1992 [1899], p. 26)*

If the children in the book are not actually shown reading in the stories, they have certainly read a lot. 'Good Hunting', pivots on knowledge of Kipling's *The Jungle Book*; in 'Being Detectives' Oswald mentions Sherlock Holmes, Kipling, while (Émile) Gaboriau, creator of the detective Lecoq (also referenced by Holmes himself) appears in:

> the yellow-covered books with pictures outside that are so badly printed; and you get them for fourpence-halfpenny at the bookstall where the corners of them are beginning to curl up and get dirty, with people looking to see how the story ends when they are waiting for trains. I think this is most unfair to the boy at the bookstall.
>
> *(Nesbit 1992 [1899], p. 35)*

In *The Wouldbegoods* (1901) the children build their playing around *The Pilgrim's Progress* and *The Canterbury Tales*; Oswald is sent to bed and reads *The Last of the Mohicans* (Nesbit 1992 [1901], p. 476). *The Wouldbegoods* also includes a remarkably forthright criticism of a living author, S. R. Crockett and his *The Surprising Adventures of Sir Toady Lion* (1898). Oswald notes: 'It is the only decent book I have ever read written by *Toady Lion's* author. The others are mere piffle. But many people like them' (p. 255).

Nesbit's *The Railway Children* (1906) is a word and book-oriented book: words are power. The mother's knowledge of French helps to save the Russian stranger who had 'written beautiful books', and writing becomes a feminist issue:

> 'And then will Mother go on writing again?' asked Peter.
> 'We shall see,' said the old gentleman with a slight, swift glance at Bobbie; 'perhaps something nice may happen and she won't have to.'
> 'I love my writing,' said Mother, very quickly.
>
> *(Nesbit 1991 [1906], p. 171)*

Rudyard Kipling also got himself into trouble with a (just) living author, Frederic W. Farrar, in his passionate satire on the school story, *Stalky and Co* (1899). His characters have read Farrar's *Eric, or Little by Little* (1868) and *St Winifred's: or, The World of School* (1862) and they don't think much of them:

> 'He read "Eric, or Little by Little,"' said M'Turk; 'so we gave him "St. Winifred's, or the World of School." They spent all their spare time stealing at St. Winifred's, when they weren't praying or getting drunk at pubs ...'.
>
> *(Kipling 1987a [1899], p. 50)*

> It was a maiden aunt of Stalky who sent him both books, with the inscription, 'To dearest Artie, on his sixteenth birthday;' ... it was Beetle, returned from Bideford, who flung them on the window-sill of Number Five study with news that Bastable would advance but ninepence on the two; "Eric; or, Little by Little," being almost as great a drug as "St. Winifred's." ... And as they ought to have been at a house cricket-match, they began to renew their acquaintance, intimate and unholy, with the volumes.
>
> 'Here we are!' said M'Turk. '"Corporal punishment produced on Eric the worst effects. He burned not with remorse or regret"—make a note o' that, Beetle—"but with shame and violent indignation. He glared"—oh, naughty Eric! Let's get to where he goes in for drink.'
>
> 'Hold on half a shake. Here's another sample. "The Sixth," he says, "is the palladium of all public schools." But this lot'—Stalky rapped the gilded book—'can't prevent fellows drinkin', and stealin', an' lettin' fags out of window at night, an' – an' doin' what they please. Golly, what we've missed—not goin' to St. Winifred's! ...'.
>
> *(p. 61)*

Kipling's *Puck of Pook's Hill* (1906) is based on an element of *Midsummer Night's Dream*; the main child-characters, Dan and Una name their favourite place 'Volaterrae' from *Lays of Ancient Rome* (Kipling 1987b [1906], p. 118) know their books of ballads (p. 167) and read Longfellow: 'The bell rang for tea faintly across the meadows. Dan lay in the bows of the *Golden Hind*; Una in the stern, the book of verses open in her lap, was reading from "The Slave's Dream"' (p. 115). The thwarting of a plot to invade England at Pevensey depends on reading and writing. When the (illiterate) Norman knight de Aquila has the written confession from the traitor Fulke in his hands, he says, '"Bones of the saints ... The pen cuts deep. I could never have fetched that grunt out of thee with any sword"' (p. 113). Even the title of the sequel, *Rewards and Fairies*, comes from a popular poem by Richard Corbet, part of which the children sing in the book (p. 209).

Books in books, then, were taken as read – but it is Arthur Ransome, a pivotal figure in children's literature (he has been credited with inventing the 'summer holidays' and democratising adventure stories) whose books epitomise the idea of the child reader in the book. They demonstrate most clearly the value that the culture set upon reading, and the *naturalness* of the relation between life, fiction and fiction within fiction which might be the envy of literacy teachers today.

His characters are deeply imbued with their reading – it enriches and underpins their adventures at almost every point. They name the books that influence them, and play with the contents of those books; there is also the assumption of shared reading with the audience; and, behind that, shared cultural assumptions and shared literary-generic assumptions (or, at least, the assumption that it is normal to pass these on through books). Although occasionally this might seem didactic, Ransome's remarkable empathy with his characters (adult as well as child) strongly suggests that he was writing the world as he knew it, and his readers as he knew them, rather than the world as he would have liked it to be, or his readers as he might have wished them to be.

The epigraph to Chapter 1 one of *Swallows and Amazons* (1930), 'The Peak in Darien' is from Keats's 'On first looking into Chapman's Homer':

> 'Or like stout Cortez, when with eagle eyes,
> He stared at the Pacific – and all his men
> Looked at each other with a wild surmise –
> Silent, upon a peak in Darien'.
>
> (p. 15)

This is, later, partially explained:

> And it was then, when they first stood on the cliff and looked out over mile upon mile of water, that Titty had given the place its name. She had heard the sonnet read aloud at school, and forgotten everything in it except the pic-ture of the explorers looking at the Pacific Ocean for the first time.
>
> *(p. 17)*

When the children are provisioning *Swallow*, there is an example not only of named books, but the fine line that the children walk (especially Titty) between fantasy and reality (and also a point about gender roles and reading):

> They also put in the ship's library. Titty had found on the shelves in the parlour a German Dictionary left by some former visitor. 'It's full of foreign language,' she said, 'and we shall want it for talking with the natives.' In the end it was left behind, because it was large and heavy, and also it might be the wrong language. Instead, Titty took *Robinson Crusoe*. 'It tells you just what to do on an island,' she said. John took *The Seaman's Handybook*, and Part Three of *The Baltic Pilot* [Admiralty Sailing Directions, reissued 2010 by the British Library]. Both books had belonged to his father, but John took them with him even on holidays. Mate Susan took *Simple Cooking for Small Households*.
>
> *(p. 33)*

When Titty is left alone on the island, there is a page devoted to *Robinson Crusoe*, quoting paragraphs on his sleeping in trees because of ravenous beasts, and teaching the parrot to speak (p. 220).

In *Winter Holiday* (1933) the children re-name the houseboat the *Fram* after Nansen's ship: books provide the motivation for the plot:

> Dorothea was a little disappointed in the books. She, Titty, and Dick began at once to search along the two shelves that held Captain Flint's houseboat library. All the books seemed to be books of travel. Dorothea had been looking for stories, but there were none except *The Riddle of the Sands*, and that, when she glanced at the charts in the beginning of it, did not seem her sort of book. But Dick had found almost at once the very book he wanted.
>
> 'Here it is,' he said. '*Farthest North. The Voyage and Exploration of the* Fram, *and the Fifteen-Months Sledge Expedition*. This'll tell us everything we want to know.'
>
> *(p. 83)*

Ransome derives a good deal of gentle humour from this contrast, and without Dorothea's literary-historical interests, *The Picts and the Martyrs* (1943) would hardly have a plot at all. Books dominate the second chapter, as Dick and Dorothea travel north by train:

> Dick had opened his suitcase and taken out a thin blue book, *Sailing*, by E. F. Knight, on which he meant to put some hard work during the journey.
>
> 'What are the other books?' asked Dorothea.
>
> '*Pocket Book of Birds*,' said Dick, 'and *Common Objects of the Countryside* ...'.
>
> 'Oh,' said Dorothea. 'Nothing to read at all ... I'm half way through *The Sea Hawk*' [Sabatini, 1915] ... As the train slowed down for the last time, Dorothea closed *The Sea Hawk* with a sigh.
>
> 'It all came right in the end,' she said. 'The horrid brother had to own up and everyone knew Sir Oliver wasn't a murderer ...'.
>
> *(pp. 15, 16)*

Similarly, the plot of *The Big Six* (1940) hinges on the application of Dorothea's fiction-based idea of detection to 'reality' – initially to the bewilderment of the pragmatic village boys:

> 'All the world believed them guilty,' said Dorothea. 'Their fathers' and their mother's [sic] grey hairs went down in sorrow to their graves ... The villain fights like a rat once he's cornered.'
>
> Bill, despairing of Dorothea, turned to Tom. 'We ain't none of us villains,' he said. 'You know that.'
>
> *(pp. 185–186)*

And later:

> 'But what if he gets caught?' [said Dorothea] 'The river's so handy. A splash …
> A groan … Just a few bubbles in the dark …'.
> 'There'd be more'n a few bubbles if anyone push Tom Dudgeon in the
> river,' … said Pete.
>
> *(p. 339)*

Ransome distinguishes gender in his in-book child readers: there is a clear, and essentially realistic distinction between the practical books chosen by the males, John and Dick (and the proto-male, Susan), and the romances chosen by the females, Titty and Dorothea. This reflects a gender divide which has echoed through education and literacy studies – notably in books such as Elaine Millard's *Differently Literate* (1997) – girls read more, and more fiction than boys. As Ransome's books demonstrate, 'Authority … is located within male culture … On the other hand, the creative process may be inscribed within the feminine, particularly in its most expressive and experimental forms' (Millard 1997, pp. 15, 28). But there is also an acceptance of the cheerful rejection of books by the outgoing characters, Nancy and Roger, or the pragmatic working-classes, Bill and Pete. What distinguishes Ransome is that neither the bookish nor the non-bookish can succeed alone: book-reading is essential to the success of the team.

Perhaps the most interesting moments are when Ransome doesn't feel that he has to name the texts his characters reference. In *Swallowdale* (1931), he assumes that his readers will know (Felicia Hemans's) *Casabianca*, which Nancy and Peggy have to recite. On the top of 'Kanchenjunga' (aka The Old Man of Coniston) (subject of four high-profile climbing attempts between 1929 and 1931), Ransome describes the vista in words taken virtually *verbatim* from Wordsworth's *The Prelude* ('beyond range after range of low hills, the land ended and the sea began, the real sea…'); then Titty, seeing Skiddaw in the distance says

> 'Where's Carlisle? … It must be somewhere over there.'
> 'How do you know?' asked Nancy.
> '"And the red glare on Skiddaw woke [sic] the burghers of Carlisle" [The final lines of Macaulay's 'The Armada']. Probably in those days they didn't have blinds in bedroom windows.'
> 'We know that one, too,' said Peggy. 'But not all of it. It's worse than "Casabianca"'.
>
> *(p. 335)*

Other children's novels of the period show a similar preoccupation. Every chapter epigraph for Pamela Whitlock and Katharine Hull's *The Far Distant Oxus* (1936) is from Matthew Arnold's *Sohrab and Rustum*, while the power of literacy is demonstrated in Geoffrey Trease's *Bows Against the Barons* (1936):

Dickon produced a letter from his wallet and his host smoothed it out on the table. He read it slowly, his bushy eyebrows knitted, his long forefinger spelling out the words. Dickon, who could not read, watched and wondered how these black scrawls and lines could possibly carry Robin's words to the weaver.

(p. 35)

In the immediate post-second world war period, in which British authors tended to look back to a pre-war golden age, Arrietty in Mary Norton's *The Borrowers* (1952) has a library: 'This was a set of those miniature volumes which the Victorians loved to print, but which to Arrietty seemed the size of very large church bibles ... [Her favourite was] Bryce's *Tom Thumb Diary and Proverb Book*' (Norton 2007 [1952], p. 14). When it rains at the Professor's house in C. S. Lewis's *The Lion, the Witch and the Wardrobe* (1950), Susan Pevensey observes: 'we're pretty well off. There's a wireless and lots of books' (Lewis 2009 [1950], pp. 11–12). Philippa Pearce's *Tom's Midnight Garden* (1958) appropriately enough for a very ambivalent book, has an ambivalent attitude to books. The bored and over-fed Tom

at first tried to read himself to sleep with Aunt Gwen's schoolgirl stories. They did not even bore him enough for that; but he persevered with them. Then Uncle Alan found him reading at half past eleven at night. There had been an outcry. After that Tom was rationed to ten minutes reading in bed ... He did not regret the reading, but the dragging hours seemed longer in the dark.

(p. 10)

But more generally, fiction of the post-war period seemed to have turned away from books and bookishness. Apart from neo-conservative hangovers like Matilda, or Richard Adams's *Watership Down*'s (1972) pretentious display of chapter epigraphs, perhaps the day of the book as an approved element of books, let alone inter-*book* reference was fading. Joan Aiken's *The Wolves of Willoughby Chase* (1962), written by an author from a very bookish background, fails to include readers and books; E. L. Konigsburg's *From the Mixed-Up Files of Mrs Basil E. Frankweiler* (1967) is an outstanding example of the 'smart kids' novels of the 1960s and 1970s and yet when the child characters do encounter books – for research purposes – they soon get bored.

It can be argued that since the 1950s, with the gradual inundation of communication by television and, later, computing and the Internet, that the position of reading fiction (and especially the reading of books) in the cultural/educational world has shifted. Intertextuality has not diminished, but its connections have changed: the impact of digital media has not altered the degree of studiousness portrayed in books (or texts in general), but its significance may be different. Is the kind of literacy that the image of the child reading *in* the book endorses in decline?

We may ask why, in this electronic, post-literate world, should we valorise book-narrative, or one kind of reading? Is the old, linear, static, book-bound, total-absorption way of reading still valid as a model for twenty-first century 'literacy'?

Are we simply maintaining assumptions about the innate virtue/necessity of shaping experience through hard-copy- (or electronic simulacra-) transmitted narrative devices/patterns/tropes for ideological reasons? After all, is the transmission of schemas for understanding a certain type of literary and cultural literacy no more than an attempt to perpetuate it? Perhaps it is time to change.

Or, as seems at least equally probable, as long as books are written, they will be written by book people – people with faith in the book as book. In any case, as will be seen from other chapters, the child reading *in* the book is alive and well – although she/he may be seen more in picturebooks or science fiction or fantasy (such as Cornelia Funke's *Inkheart* (2003)) than before.

Whatever the truth, readers in books continue to maintain a dialogue both inside and outside the books about the nature and validity of books themselves. Oswald Bastable's ironic doubts about the usefulness, or at least the truth of books have not gone away. One of the most serious and articulate contributions to the debate has come from Terry Pratchett. In the first of his *Discworld* novels marketed for younger readers, *The Amazing Maurice and his Educated Rodents* (2001), Pratchett led a great deal of fun with a girl who knows her folk-tales:

> 'Probably belonged to a witch, I expect with a name like Griselda or one of those names … who lived in a gingerbread cottage in the forest, probably.'
>
> 'Yeah, right, Griselda, right,' said Maurice. And then, because he wouldn't be Maurice if he couldn't be a bit inventive, he added, 'Only it was a crispbread cottage, 'cos she was slimming. Very healthy witch, Griselda.'
>
> The girl looked puzzled for a moment. 'That's not how it should go,' she said.
>
> *(p. 64)*

But as is usual with Pratchett, the discussion can be deadly serious (see Arizpe in this volume). In *The Wee Free Men* (2003), the apprentice witch, Tiffany, is thinking about an old woman, Mrs Snapperley, who had been driven out of her cottage, on suspicion of being a witch, and died. Tiffany sits in the three-hole privy with a book:

> Tiffany lit the candle, made herself comfortable, and looked at the book of Faerie Tales … .She'd never really liked the book. It seemed to her that it tried to tell her what to do and what to think. Don't stray from the path, don't open that door, but hate the wicked witch because she is *wicked*. … The stories *weren't real*. But Mrs Snapperley had died because of stories.
>
> *(pp. 62–63)*

Plus ça change … Perhaps, after all, the self-endorsement of the reader and writer by building themselves into their own fictions is inevitable, and whatever the whirl of changing media and changing concepts of literacy, the core image of the child-and-the-book in the book will never be totally lost.

Primary sources

Alcott, Louisa M. *Little Women* [1868 in two volumes; 1880 in one]. London: Puffin, 1953.

Dahl, Roald. *Matilda* [1988]. London: Puffin, 1989.

Dahl, Roald. *The Complete Adventures of Charlie and Mr Willy Wonka* [1964 *Charlie and the Chocolate Factory*; 1972 *Charlie and the Great Glass Elevator*]. London: Puffin, 2001.

Garner, Alan. "The Stone Book." *The Stone Book Quartet* [1976]. London: HarperCollins, 1992.

Hodgson Burnett, Frances. *A Little Princess* [1905]. Ed. U. C. Knoepflmacher. New York: Penguin, 2002.

Hodgson Burnett, Frances. *Little Lord Fauntleroy* [1886]. Ed. Dennis Butts. Oxford: Oxford University Press, 1993.

Hodgson Burnett, Frances. *The Secret Garden* [1911]. Ed. Peter Hunt. Oxford: Oxford University Press, 2011.

Jefferies, Richard. *Bevis. The Story of a Boy* [1882]. Ed. Peter Hunt. Oxford: Oxford University Press, 1989.

Kipling, Rudyard. *Puck of Pook's Hill* [1906]. Ed. Sarah Wintle. London: Penguin, 1987b.

Kipling, Rudyard. *Stalky and Co* [1899]. Harmondsworth: Puffin, 1987a.

Lewis, C. S. *The Lion, the Witch and the Wardrobe* [1950]. London: HarperCollins, 2009.

Nesbit, E. *The Complete Adventures of the Treasure Seekers* [1899 *The Story of the Treasure Seekers*; 1901 *The Wouldbegoods*; 1904 *The New Treasure Seekers*]. London: Puffin, 1992.

Nesbit, E. *The Railway Children* [1906]. Ed. Dennis Butts. Oxford: Oxford University Press, 1991.

Norton, Mary. *The Complete Borrowers* [1952]. *The Borrowers*; 1955 *The Borrowers Afield*; 1959 *The Borrowers Afloat*; 1961 *The Borrowers Aloft*; 1982 *The Borrowers Avenged*; 1966 *Poor Stainless*]. London: Puffin, 2007.

Pearce, Philippa. *Tom's Midnight Garden* [1958]. London: Puffin, 1993.

Pratchett, Terry. *The Amazing Maurice and his Educated Rodents*. London: Doubleday, 2001.

Pratchett, Terry. *The Wee Free Men*. London: Doubleday, 2003.

Ransome, Arthur. *Swallowdale*. London: Cape, 1931.

Ransome, Arthur. *Swallows and Amazons*. London: Cape, 1930.

Ransome, Arthur. *The Big Six*. London: Cape, 1940.

Ransome, Arthur. *The Picts and the Martyrs*. London: Cape, 1943.

Ransome, Arthur. *Winter Holiday* [1933]. London: Cape, 1961.

Trease, Geoffrey. *Bows against the Barons* [1934]. London: Hodder and Stoughton, 1979.

Secondary sources

Benton, Michael and Fox, Geoff. *Teaching Literature 9–14*. Oxford: Oxford University Press, 1985. Print.

Chambers, Aidan. *Reading Talk*. South Woodchester: Thimble Press, 2001. Print.

Meek, Margaret. *How Texts Teach What Readers Learn*. South Woodchester: Thimble Press, 1988. Print.

Millard, Elaine. *Differently Literate*. London: Falmer Press, 1997. Print.

Sturrock, Daniel. *Storyteller. The Authorised Biography of Roald Dahl*. New York: Simon & Schuster, 2010. Print.

3

ALL FOR LOVE

The relationship between love-stories and reading as a cultural activity

Kimberley Reynolds

Leon Garfield's *The Book Lovers* (1976) is one of a cluster of books for adolescents that feature characters who are skilful and committed readers and who are also successful in love. The combination is far from typical. As other contributors to this volume have noted, although writers and publishers make their living by appealing to readers, children's literature is curiously ambivalent in its attitude to and depiction of reading as an activity, and perhaps particularly so in relation to love. Most children's books that contain a love story perpetuate the stereotype of the romantic inadequacies of the 'bluestocking' [intellectual/reading] girl and the 'nerdy' [intellectual/usually non-athletic] boy reader. In the group of books considered here, however, such characters are depicted as admirable lovers. As will be shown, they are also ambassadors for literary culture.

Books about adolescent reader-lovers share a set of values and attitudes about books and reading that make them cohere as a subgenre. These values are conveyed in three ways. First, books about reader-lovers specifically address an audience of skilled and enthusiastic readers – which generally means excluding casual readers since those without a literary hinterland are unlikely to be able to follow or respond to the literary references and assumptions about the importance of reading that are central to the texts. Next, these books use love-stories and an assumed love of reading as the hook to expand readers' knowledge about literature: how genres work, for instance, or knowledge of classic/classical texts and characters, or aspects of literary tradition. Finally, and largely through this mixture of address and instruction in literary tradition, they play with, but ultimately perpetuate, ideas about reading as a cultural activity that have been in circulation at least since the beginnings of the novel and the rise of reading as a form of mass recreation. In fact, as is evident in *The Book Lovers*, some aspects of being a reader-lover have ancient roots.

The paucity of children's books about readers who successfully negotiate the stages of courtship dates back to the earliest days of juvenile publishing when avid, emotionally engaged readers tended to be discredited through association with those from parts of the population that lacked social power and education. Typically, such readers consisted of the poor, children, and females. Good readers were identified with largely masculine attributes including being well-educated, rational rather than emotional, and highly discriminating about what they read. Discrediting immersive reading was part of what Deidre Shauna Lynch has identified as a deliberate strategy by those who saw themselves as the guardians of culture to demonstrate that only they had the ability to read wisely and well. For those without their training, they warned, reading could be damaging and should be avoided (Lynch 1998, pp. 146–147). This message was not unique to children's books of course: Jane Austen's novels frequently feature young women such as Marianne Dashwood and Catherine Moorland whose reading leads to significant errors in judgement. Nevertheless, because reading tends to be a skill acquired in childhood, warnings about its misuse were often directed at children, and especially girls. Indeed, when thinking about how readers are depicted in juvenile stories about love, it is important to keep in mind that when the novel as a literary form was taking shape, it was widely assumed that indulging a taste for empathetic reading would make a girl too imaginative, highly strung and unreliable to win the love of a good man.

Reading as such was not identified as problematic; rather, the fault lay in the wrong kind of readers reading the wrong kind of works in the wrong ways. Sarah Fielding's Preface to *The Governess; or, the Little Female Academy* (1749) begs readers to 'stop a Moment … to consider … what is the true Use of Reading'. The true Use of Reading, she explains, is 'to make you wise and better' and the right kind of reading results in 'both Profit and Pleasure'. When girl readers get into romantic difficulties, therefore, it is always because they have not learned the 'true Use of Reading'. They may have found reading pleasurable, but instead of making them wise it has misled them. Jackie Horne (2011) discusses Fielding's ideas about girls and reading and provides a detailed discussion of the fates of several over-empathetic girl readers in early fiction.

Variations on this theme recur across children's publishing until well into the twentieth century. As part of becoming women worthy of love, characters such as Jo March (*Little Women*, 1868–1869), Katy Carr (*What Katy Did*, 1872), and Anne Shirley (*Anne of Green Gables*, 1908) are required to outgrow the precocious, overly involved and romantic reading selves readers first meet. None of these books is primarily a love-story, however; indeed each of the girls initially spurns the idea of love and, in the cases of Jo and Anne, the young men who care for them. By the closing decades of the last century a notable change had occurred. *The Book Lovers* sets the pattern for a small but coherent sub-genre featuring adolescent readers for whom books prove to be good guides to love and a love-story draws the books' readers into the world of literature.

Love in the library

Garfield's story features a student of literature who is smitten with the attractive young librarian who issues his books each day. He is not alone: all the males in the library, from schoolboys to musty old scholars, are attracted to her, and she is practised at rebuffing their advances. What sets the young man apart is his sudden realisation that he is a reader, she is a reader, and they are surrounded by books containing famous lovers who can speak on his behalf. Under the pretext that he is collecting material for an anthology of love scenes, the student asks the librarian to help him locate suitable extracts. Initially she remains 'as dispassionate as an index': "Prose or poetry, sir? Proposals or consummations? Letters or dialogues? First love or mature passion …?" (p. 9), she asks. Undaunted, he perseveres, and knowing that he has a schoolboy rival in the library, explains that he is after 'adult' material: 'Scenes between grown men and women' (p. 9). Clearly with a view to discouraging him, the librarian directs him to a passage that readers who consult the list of extract-sources at the back of the book will find comes from Anthony Trollope's *Can You Forgive Her?* The situation, she assures him, "could scarcely be more adult" (p. 9). Set in the 1860s, the scene features 'a mature and attractive widow' who has two 'most urgent lovers – one of whom has reached boiling point in his desire for her' (p. 9). The example is not encouraging: the elderly lover is a badly dressed farmer who makes a fool of himself and is rejected following a proposal that the widow refers to as "a farce" (p. 10).

The young man cannot help but recognise the pointed nature of the extract: 'had he really been so unmitigated and ridiculous a pest as the unlucky Mr. Cheesacre?' (p. 15), he asks himself. Despite this unpromising beginning, the student perseveres. When he asks which of the men the widow marries, Garfield's literary honey-trap is set, since readers are likely to share his curiosity and so must follow the advice he is given by his *inamorata*: "Read the book," she tells him, 'but not quite so unkindly as perhaps might have been expected' (p. 15). Realising his mistake in asking for something about mature love, the student thinks he is on the right track when the librarian suggests something more 'tender'. "How well you understand me" he exclaims. "I understand you all right" she replies, before setting off to find him extract number two (p. 15). It too turns out to be exactly what she has promised, though again not at all what the student had in mind.

The young man's spirit and the extent of his literary knowledge start to be displayed when he begins to counter with selections of his own (proving him to be a knowledgeable and attentive reader), which do not always show her in quite the light she expects. Soon *The Book Lovers* is using love as a hook for pulling readers through a survey of sixteen classic texts written by authors from Jane Austen to W. H. Auden and encompassing French and Russian writers in translation. Garfield's selection also subtly teaches readers about form, style, and the development of European literature. For example, the relationship between the student and his librarian reworks that of the lover and his lady found in the eleventh-century phenomenon known as courtly love. Courtly love was itself a literary invention which popularised a set of amatory rituals that, according to C. S. Lewis's *The Allegory of Love* (1936), continued to influence how romantic love was written about and understood for at least 800 years (Lewis 1977 [1936]). Garfield's collection appeared 40 years after Lewis made that claim; evidence that by then the tradition had lasted almost another half century. For example, Garfield endows his student with many of the characteristics of the courtly lover, starting with the way he periodically torments himself with the idea that his cause is doomed because his beloved is superior to him and so unattainable.

As in the case of the first courtly lovers, readers are encouraged to regard the young man's condition as ennobling, since in striving to demonstrate his worth and win her love he is cultivating and displaying such admirable qualities as courage, modesty, humility, generosity, loyalty and wit. The ability to woo through word-play is another identifying feature of the courtly lover as is a tendency to luxuriate in the idea of and emotions attendant upon being in love. Garfield's student displays all of these ways of behaving. Courtly love is a kind of self-indulgent game, however, and so neither the stuff of a satisfying love story nor of a sound literary education. For this reason, courtly love is where Garfield's reader-lover begins, but as the book starts to draw on texts that are more psychologically complex, so the student's character develops and he becomes a more beguiling and effective wooer. It transpires that the librarian has not been unaffected by their literary duel, and to provide the happy ending of a true romance she signals that she has dismantled her defences when she gives him her final extract. This is inevitably part of the scene in *Pride and Prejudice* (1813) in which Mr. Darcy confesses his attachment to Elizabeth Bennet for a second time and she, 'immediately, though not very fluently, gave him to understand, that her sentiments had undergone so material a change, since the period to which he alluded, as to make her receive with gratitude and pleasure, his present assurance' (2007 [1813], p. 132).

Despite this apparently satisfactory conclusion to their literary courtship, *The Book Lovers* ends on a note of caution which brings the readings into the twentieth century. The final extract in the volume is presented to the pair by an elderly scholar who has been observing their progress. He has copied out W. H. Auden's 'The Willow Wren and the Stare' (1953) in which a pair of birds listen as a young man seduces a girl with pretty words. She consents; he is 'utterly content'. But the final lines cast doubt on what has passed between them:

> She laughed, he laughed, they laughed together,
> Then they ate and drank:
> *Did he know what he meant?* Said the willow-wren –
> *God only knows*, said the stare.

Doubts about the future of the lovers bring together the realms and conventions of courtly love and children's literature. Where Auden implies his couple have had sex (the young man expresses his contentment on waking in the arms of the girl),

Garfield, in accordance with the rules of both courtly love and children's literature, stays in the world of words and desires. Because the beloved was often socially superior and/or already married, courtly love was rarely consummated. When it was, the pleasure was invariably short-lived; in the most famous models of courtly love, Guinevere and Lancelot, Tristan and Isolde and, later, Romeo and Juliet, physical lovemaking brings tragic consequences. A similar pattern for long pertained in Young Adult fiction, which tended to discourage readers from acting on their desires by focusing on the possible consequences – pregnancy, disease, and disrupted education among them (see Trites, 2004).

The uses of romantic fiction

Although *The Book Lovers* stays safely within the traditions of courtly love, subsequent books featuring adolescent reader-lovers are more inclined to trust characters who have done their homework by studying love on the page before moving on to real life. An unusual example is found in Diana Wynne Jones's *Fire and Hemlock* (1985), in which grown-up Tom cultivates child Polly's taste in literature by sending her boxes of books to mark holidays and special occasions. This is the device Jones uses to broaden readers' literary tastes and knowledge. Like Sarah Fielding, Tom believes that there is a 'true Use of Reading' and that it can only be gained from good books. There is also, however, an ulterior motive behind the selection of myths, ballads, legends and children's fantasies he sends Polly. They have been chosen to cultivate the heroic qualities he needs his future lover to possess, for unbeknownst to her, Polly must play Janet to his Tam Lin, and save him from the deadly clutches of the Faerie Queene. By the time *Fire and Hemlock* reaches its frenetic conclusion, Polly is reading English Literature at University. It is she who becomes the reader-lover of the story; to what she has learned from the books Tom gave her in childhood she adds her own knowledge of modern writers such as T. S. Eliot (who, of course, references ancient works) and solves the problem of how to defeat the current incarnation of the Faerie Queene, and her scheme to take Tom to pay her tithe to Hell.

Diana Wynne Jones's Young Adult novels are richly intertextual and committed to fostering a love of books and literary tradition in her readers, but the writer who more than any other does this through the device of having adolescent readers become lovers is Margaret Mahy. Mahy's writing regularly defies Trites's contention that Young Adult fiction is characterised by the urge to curb the power of the rising generation on the part of its writers and gatekeepers. In novels such as *The Tricksters* (1986), *Alchemy* (2002) and *24 Hours* (2004) she positively celebrates the coming into power, including sexual power, associated with adolescence. All Mahy's books are steeped in literary references and her characters are often already actively developing their knowledge of literature, but two books stand out for their use of reader-lovers. In *The Changeover* (1984), teenage witch, Sorry Carlisle, is one of those who initially misunderstands the 'true Use of Reading'. He is a dedicated reader of romance fiction, not, it seems, for its own sake, but because he hopes it will teach him how to captivate girls. Like Garfield and Jones, Mahy is intent upon introducing readers to high-quality writing and steering them away from books that are banal and badly written, so it quickly becomes clear that Sorry's diet of bodice rippers has been feeding and perverting his already predatory attitude to girls, and that he has learned nothing useful from them in terms of attracting the opposite sex. As in all the other books discussed in this chapter (and all the books in the subset of children's books about reader-lovers), the character with whom Sorry falls in love is associated with quality literature as represented by long-established genres and conventions. Laura Chant, whose mother works in a bookshop, makes it clear that she despises his taste in books. As Laura and Sorry grow closer, he stops reading romance and starts responding to the clues from other genres (fairy tale, hero-quest, and myth among them) that enable the young couple to save Laura's little brother from a deadly possession.

A very different pair of reader-lovers is featured in Mahy's *The Catalogue of the Universe* (1985), a retelling (among other texts) of 'The Frog Prince' in which the prince is Tycho Potter. Tycho is clever and extremely well read, in part because he uses his command of information as a form of social currency to compensate for the fact that he is small and peculiar looking. Reading also serves to distract him from the fear that his looks mean he will never be a success with girls. Like Sorry Carlisle, Tycho and his best friend, Angela, have been reading romantic novels to find out about love. But unlike Sorry, they are eclectic readers who discuss and compare what they read, and so they recognise the limitations of such works. Reading is what unites the two. It is Angela who has given Tycho the book that lends its title to Mahy's novel: *The Catalogue of the Universe*, a reference work about the night sky to complement Tycho's fascination with astronomy. Tycho's preoccupation with the heavens is associated with his feelings for Angela, whose name in his mind at least is connected to celestial bodies. Angela is beautiful and popular at school, and Tycho's idealisation and elevation of her signal that she is the lady to his courtly lover. This role is never overtly enacted, however, as Tycho keeps his feelings well hidden.

He may be the courtly lover, but Tycho is also the frog prince to Angela's princess. Angela has been raised by her mother, Dido. Queen Dido is remembered for her ill-fated love for Aneas, so readers who know that story are not surprised to learn that Angela's mother has also been abandoned by the man she loved. In this case, however, Dido has turned the story of her ill-fated romance into the fairy tale of Angela's life: "Remember you used to tell me about my father when I was a little girl, just as if it was a fairy-story," Angela prompts her at a crucial moment in the story. "It was," said Dido, nodding. "It really was" (p. 7). This is the point when Mahy shifts the narrative mode from fairy tale to detective story. Angela sets about tracking her father down with a view to reuniting her parents, only to learn that the story was not quite as her mother had told it. At this point the narrative again switches genres, though whether its register is gothic or tragic is not initially clear.

Losing the story of her princess self unmakes Angela, who runs off into the night. Dido and Tycho misread the events and do so with specific reference to books and reading. Dido is concerned that Angela will attempt to harm herself, as she explains to Tycho:

> "I think I ought to ring the police. You and she are always making fun of romance, I know, but really you're both riddled with it – and it's romantic to write yourself off under certain circumstances".
>
> *(p. 117)*

In fact, Angela's dark night of the soul opens her eyes to what is genuinely important in her life – her mother and Tycho. In the middle of the night, the bedraggled teenager appears at Tycho's to find him consulting *The Catalogue of the Universe* and studying the sky through his telescope (symbolising the fact that he is searching for her). Once she has made her version of the Elizabeth Bennet declaration, the book is swiftly put to a more practical use when Tycho stands on it so they are the same height when they kiss. "I always knew that was a good book," he observes, showing a flash of the courtly lover's wit (p. 135).

Dido's broken relationship was founded on the kinds of popular myths and images that circulate around love. At one level, the book warns that love-stories can be dangerous stuff. But as in Garfield and Jones, the problem is not with what is read but how, and specifically with confusing life and fiction. Having taken in so many stories and experimented with different ways of reading them, Angela and Tycho have mastered the 'true Use of Reading'. When Tycho stands on *The Catalogue of the Universe*, he is metaphorically standing on all the books he has read. From books Angela has learned how to value their relationship, seeing Tycho properly rather than in the guise of her funny-looking frog-friend, and Tycho has learned not to let self-consciousness prevent him from being kissed into his princely condition. Books have served exactly the purpose Sarah Fielding describes: both teenagers are wiser and better people because of their reading. More than that, reading has empowered them and given them the story patterns and vocabularies that will help them collaborate on creating their own new story.

The subgenre continues to grow and, perhaps surprisingly in this sexually informed and mediatised age, to gain in popularity. Recent additions to books about adolescent reader-lovers include Stephen Chbosky's *The Perks of Being a Wallflower* (1999) and John Green's *The Fault in Our Stars* (2012). Unlike the other books discussed here, Chbosky's and Green's books are bestsellers and have been released as commercial films. Their popularity owes much to their emotionally loaded plotlines which, in the case of Green, slip into mawkish sentiment. Nevertheless, both show characters who read as witty and brave, empathetic, insightful, creative, trustworthy and, despite a few twists, successful in love. In *The Perks of Being a Wallflower*, Charlie negotiates what turn out to be three interlinked traumas – the death of his much-loved aunt, the suicide of a classmate, and realising that his aunt sexually abused him – through a course of independent reading set for him by his English teacher. The 'introduction to literature' component of the story takes the form of the teacher's recommendations (*On the Road*,

The Naked Lunch, *The Stranger*, *This Side of Paradise*, *Peter Pan*, *A Separate Peace*, *To Kill a Mockingbird*, *The Catcher in the Rye*, *Hamlet*, *Walden* and *The Great Gatsby*). The book is punctuated with essays about his reading that also follow Charlie's integration into a new group of slightly older, more worldly and creative friends. Largely through these new friends his reading is respected but also augmented with aspects of youth culture, notably rock music and *The Rocky Horror Show*. He also watches film and television, and references to books and media run through the novel and add to its sense. This is not the kind of demanding intertextuality found in Jones and Mahy; nevertheless, reading is crucial to the unfolding of the narrative and Charlie's reading gives him ideas and insights his new friends find attractive. He makes them gifts of the books in token of his love for them as a group. They show their love by giving him a typewriter and helping him realise himself as a writer.

Charlie loves his new set of friends, but he also falls in love with Sam, one of the girls in it. After some confused signals, Charlie eventually wins Sam and all should end happily. By the end of the twentieth century, in Young Adult books acknowledging mutual love and attraction tends to end with a scene in which the relationship is consummated – and that nearly happens for Charlie and Sam. At the crucial moment, however, the legacies of abuse (which Charlie has repressed) rise to the surface and he is unable to perform sexually. This leads to a break-down following which Charlie is institutionalised. Instead of making him a failed lover, however, this is the moment when Charlie discovers how deeply he is loved – by friends (including Sam) and family. They work with him as he recovers and by the end of the book he is ready to emerge as a healed figure.

Unlike earlier books about reader-lovers, *The Perks of Being a Wallflower* doesn't have a happy-ever-after romantic ending. Charlie and Sam do not become a couple. Nevertheless, there is a sense of optimism around Charlie's prospects for the future, including his future as a lover, that arise from, the reading and loving he has done. Charlie has learned to profit from his reading. True love runs a more traditional course in *The Fault in Our Stars*. As the title suggests, Hazel and Gus are star-crossed lovers. They know this, however, because they are both readers as well as cancer patients. Initially it seems the star-crossed element in their relationship lies in the fact that Gus, who has been declared cured, will have to watch Hazel die since her cancer has spread. In fact, at the end of the book his cancer returns aggressively and he predeceases her. Before that, however, they have shared an intense experience with her favourite book which is by a mysterious writer and features a girl who is dying of cancer. Hazel is frustrated because the book ends enigmatically in mid-sentence. In the role of courtly lover, Gus goes on a quest to locate the author and command his services for Hazel. He discovers that the writer lives in Amsterdam and secures funds from a cancer charity so that he and Helen can travel to Amsterdam to meet the book's author.

The reclusive writer turns out to be a disappointment, but reading and decoding the text have been a kind of literary foreplay and the teenagers have a romantic evening that ends in successful sex. Life may be short for both of them, but they have found love through a book and from a shared history of reading. The return of Gus's cancer could be seen as the kind of punishment Trites associates with Young Adult fiction, but he knew about it (and with-held that knowledge from Hazel) before they had sex, which defies Trites's pattern and changes the relationship between teenage sex and consequences. Green also changes the lot of the reader-as-lover by making the key text an invented one, and implying rather than detailing and referencing the other reading they have done. Nevertheless, the centrality of reading in Hazel and Gus's relationship is never in question. Reading has made them wiser and better.

Hazel and Gus display all the characteristics of reader-lovers – and of many lovers from literature. They are Romeo and Juliet, Anne Frank and Peter, and the tragic lovers from Eric Segal's bestselling misery-romance, *Love Story* (1970). They are witty and wise, and they woo each other thoughtfully so that the relationship proves durable. Neither illness nor death destroys it. When it comes to love, then, *The Fault in Our Stars* belongs to the subgenre of books which suggest there is much to be said for finding a lover who is also a reader, if what is read is good literature and the reader knows 'the true Use of Reading'. What that use is and what is meant by good literature have changed surprisingly little over the centuries. What is different is that the ability to read wisely and well is now associated, not with a particular class, sex or age, but with a self-identifying group of book lovers who are credited with having gained Profit as well as Pleasure from reading. Whether love could be used as a portal to literary tradition for a wider group is something that remains to be seen, though the popularity of Chboksy's and Green's books and their translation into film may be evidence that this is happening.

Primary sources

Alcott, Louisa May. *Little Women* [1868–1869 in two volumes]. London: Puffin Classics, 2011.

Auden, W. H. 'The Willow Wren and the Stare' in *Encounter* (November, 1953), pp, 13–14, accessed at http://www.unz.org/Pub/Encounter-1953nov-00013 on 1 November, 2013. Online

Austen, Jane. *Pride and Prejudice* [1813]. London: Vintage Classics, 2007.

Chbosky, Stephen. *The Perks of Being a Wallflower*. New York: Simon and Schuster, 1999.

Coolidge, Susan. *What Katy Did* [1872]. Ware, Herts: Wordsworth Children's Classics, 1994.

Fielding, Sarah. *The Governess; or, the Little Female Academy* [1749]. Ed. Candace Ward. Peterborough, Ontario: Broadview Press, 1995.

Garfield, Leon. *The Book Lovers*. London: Ward Lock, 1976.

Green, John. *The Fault in Our Stars* [2012]. London: Penguin, 2013.

Jones, Diana Wynne. *Fire and Hemlock* [1985]. London: HarperCollins, 2011.

Mahy, Margaret. *Alchemy* [2002]. New York: Simon & Schuster, 2003.

Mahy, Margaret. *The Catalogue of the Universe* [1985]. London: CollinsFlamingo, 2002.

Mahy, Margaret. *The Changeover* [1984]. London: HarperCollins, 2007.

Mahy, Margaret. *The Tricksters* [1986]. London: CollinsFlamingo, 2009.

Mahy, Margaret. *24 Hours* [2004]. London: CollinsFlamingo, 2009.

Montgomery, L. M. *Anne of Green Gables* [1908]. Ware, Herts: Wordsworth Children's Classics, 1994.

Segal, Eric. *Love Story* [1970]. London: Hodder and Stoughton, 2006.

Secondary sources

Horne, Jackie C. *History and the Construction of the Child in Early British Children's Literature.* Farnham: Ashgate, 2011. Print.

Lewis, C. S., *The Allegory of Love: A Study in Medieval Tradition* [1936]. Oxford: Oxford University Press, 1977. Print.

Lynch, Deidre Shauna. *The Economy of Character: Novels, Market Culture and the Business of Inner Meaning.* 2nd ed. Chicago: University of Chicago Press, 1998. Print.

Trites, Roberta Seelinger. *Disturbing the Universe: Power and Repression in Adolescent Fiction.* Iowa City: University of Iowa Press, 2004. Print.

PART II

Reading and its consequences

How dangerous is reading?

4

SPELLBINDING BOOKS IN YOUNG ADULT FANTASY FICTION

Maureen A. Farrell

Introduction

Fantasy fiction is an area of Young Adult literature that has shown exponential growth in recent years. Since the publication of fantasy series such as Ursula Le Guin's *The Wizard of Earthsea* or Susan Cooper's *The Dark is Rising* sequence, both of which began in the 1960s, a raft of new titles have emerged with increasing popularity for the Young Adult market. These new titles encompass all forms of fantasy from the epic or high fantasy style such as Garth Nix's *Old Kingdom* series, to modern re-envisioning of the fairy-tale like Gail Carson Levine's *Ella Enchanted* or Robin McKinley's *Beauty* and even in the form of Lemony Snicket's pastiches such as the *All the Wrong Questions* series. Central to a great deal of fantasy fiction is the presence of magic in some form or another. Whether this manifests itself in the 'real' world or some secondary or parallel world, its impact is significant and usually pivotal to the plot. A relatively common feature of magic in most cases is that it is rule bound and complex and that access to it is restricted. There are two consequences of this. One is a high instance of books that explain or codify or exemplify the magic in these novels. There are law books and lore books, spell books and enchanted books; there are books that serve as portals or keys to alternative worlds, and there are books that are actually weapons. The second consequence is that there are readers, often young people, in the novels who need to learn how to read both the books and the magic. Sanders (2009) and Nelson (2006) both note that, to date, there has been no systematic examination of the relationship between magical books and the reader/apprentice in Young Adult fantasy novels. This chapter attempts to provide it.

Magical books: why and how?

Broadly, magical books can function in one of two ways. In some instances, what matters about them is the *content*. Like the Book of Gramarye in *The Dark is Rising*, the purpose of some books is to record or transfer knowledge. Books such as these can provide an explanation of events for the characters caught up in the narrative; they might present the means of escape or become the weapon of salvation for the participants. The second volume in Nix's Old Kingdom series, *Lirael* (2001) offers many examples of such books which Lirael, in her job as a librarian, encounters. For example, there are books from which she learns magic and also the 'Book of Remembrance and Forgetting' which leads her to her new role as Remembrancer for her community. In Angie Sage's Septimus Heap series books, such as 'The Undoing of the Darkenesse' and its companion volume 'The Darke Index', actually become weapons. These books are kept separate because they are considered too dangerous when they are together. The Darke Index is used in the sixth book of the series *Darke* to create a Darke Domain. At this point the books play a critical role in the survival of the castle and its inhabitants.

There are also books which embody knowledge as power, and very often part of their power is the ability to select or restrict readership. Often, they are disguised or unrecognisable in some way and only specific characters can identify or read them. For example, in John Stephens's *The Emerald Atlas* (2011) ownership or guardianship of the atlas that is the focus of the novel changes hands several times and the fortunes of the owners rise and fall accordingly. Only once the book is in the right hands can its full power be realised and the story come to a satisfactory resolution. What is interesting here is the shift in agency: it is the reader, in the act of reading, who is able to release the power of the book, and thus access the knowledge contained in it. Without the reader, the book and its contents are diminished.

In the second category of magical books, the book is an artefact that has been imbued with magic properties. Sometimes, as in *Ella Enchanted* (2011 [1997]) for example, the fact that the artefact is a *book* doesn't seem to matter much: it is simply the item that enables Ella to keep track of her family and friends and after her marriage to keep track of her children. A magical mirror or ring would have done as well. But at best, the bookishness of the book becomes a determining feature of the magic. So, for example, a magical book might pull a reader out of his 'real' life into the fiction contained in its pages, or a character might emerge from the book and interact in the reader's 'real' world. There are a number of texts that work like this: probably the best known of these is Cornelia Funke's *Inkheart* series where characters from the 'real' world like Meggie and her father enter Inkworld, or the world of the book, while Dustfinger and Farad find themselves read out of 'Inkheart' and into the real world. Reflective, meta-fictive texts such as these challenge the reader, both the reader in the text and the reader of the text, to test the boundaries of reality and imagination, of the possible and the unlikely and the nature of fiction itself. In these cases the knowledge and understanding of books and writing is woven into the tale. Direct recognition of secondary, fictional worlds demands sophisticated understanding from the reader and an ability to make intertexual links across boundaries that are both concrete and imaginary.

Sometimes, as an extension of this exploration of reality comes an exploration of the physical potential of written language itself. In Blake Charlton's *Spellwright* (2010), for example, it is the manipulation of the language of the spell book, the incantation, that brings ideas into reality. For example, Nicodemus, the main protagonist, finds the required spell for gargoyle repair and maintenance on the pages of a codex. After writing a spell on his own hand he 'bends' his sentence into a hook and peels off the requisite paragraphs to create the crystalline lattice that is the spell. The language of the spells within the books is made real in order to be effective.

The texts which I discuss below are three contemporary Young Adult fantasy novels that all feature magical books and young readers who need to learn to read them. Each is the first volume of a trilogy, and although subsequent books develop and extend the ideas I explore here to some extent, it is the first volume of each that establishes the tropes that I wish to pursue. The books are *The Emerald Atlas* (2011) by John Stephens; *Spellwright* (2010) by Blake Charlton and Cornelia Funke's *Inkheart* (2003). These novels present contrasting propositions about books and their power. Each presents and represents books and poses questions about them, about stories, about authors, about readers and about language but in very different ways.

The Emerald Atlas

The Emerald Atlas introduces the three central characters Kate, Michael and Emma, each of whom is inextricably linked to a specific book in each text in the series. The children are orphans who have moved through different orphanages over a ten-year period. They finally end up in a mansion belonging to Dr Pym and while there they find a magical book, an atlas that grants the power of moving through time. The children have first to recognise the significance of the book and then how to activate its power. The book seems blank, but when an old photograph is touched to the page of the book the children are teleported to the time and location where the photograph was taken. In so doing they also activate a prophecy in which they have key roles. The three books they find provide the means to resolving the prophecy but, in the wrong hands, they also could become the means of utter destruction.

The atlas is one of the Books of Beginning, written by wizards at a time when the magical world and the real world were separating. The books were written to preserve magical knowledge, but the collective wisdom was split into three books in order to minimise the danger of this great knowledge falling in to the wrong hands: over time the books were lost. After a series of experiments and accidents the children come to the conclusion that the book they have really is the Atlas of Time which maps out possible pasts, presents and futures and allows movement through time and space. Kate, the oldest of the children has a particular affinity with this book and she gradually realises that when she touches a blank page of the book, even without the aid of a photograph, she 'sees' events at particular times. Not only that but the book itself seems to have bonded with her:

At its very centre, a small black dot appeared. As Kate watched it began to spread, like an ink stain. Suddenly the entire page was black. And then, she saw with horror, the blackness begin to spread up her fingers.

(The Emerald Atlas 2011, p. 91)

Kate's journey of discovery in how to both access and manage the book and its contents leads her into situations over which she seems to have little control. Her intentions may be good – to intervene in events to change their outcomes – but perhaps because her understanding of the book is incomplete, this backfires on Kate herself and the characters she tries to help. This results in consequences for all three young people, placing them in danger, separating them and ultimately teaching them about resilience, loyalty, selfishness and selflessness. It is when they are separated from their siblings that each encounter the book matched to them and the exploration of the books and their powers is made both independent and personal, as is the case for all readers of books.

In the course of the story the children begin to discern the potential of the books as keys to knowledge and discovery and also the potential for the power of their contents as weapons to destroy lives and societies. Once they recognise their unique bonds with the books they are also conscious of their own power and agency over the books' contents.

The Emerald Atlas epitomises the potential of books for both positive and negative purposes, as objects for good or as objects of power which can corrupt or indeed as objects of passive power. The book *is* a book of knowledge but it requires a 'reader' to access and animate the power. The atlas plays with the idea of both the permanence and the authority of the words on the page and proffers the notion that such books require close reading by a competent and knowing reader to get to the heart of their secrets. The book and the reader have a symbiotic relationship in this series and the outcome is dependent on both.

Spellwright

The second book offers a contrasting role for books and language as modes of magic. Charlton, a severe dyslexic, became interested in the power of conventional spelling, or, more specifically, in the effect of misspelt words on other readers. In *Spellwright* he envisions a world where the magical runes that create spells are physically forged with both brain and muscle. The magicians have to first build the spells on their own bodies using a variety of complex languages and pulling the spells out involves considerable pain. Runes must be placed in the correct order in order to create a spell. Deviation results in a "misspell" – a flawed text that behaves in an erratic, sometimes lethal, manner.

This world is home to Nicodemus Weal, an apprentice at the wizardly academy of Starhaven. Because of how fast he can forge the magical runes that create spells, Nicodemus was initially thought to be the Halcyon, a powerful spellwright prophesied to prevent an event called the War of Disjunction, which would destroy all human language. But Nicodemus has a disability, called cacography that causes him to misspell texts simply by touching them. Having failed to fulfil the prophecy Nicodemus is reduced to working for Magister Shannon, an old blind wizard who has left academic politics to care for Starhaven's lexically challenged – and thus disabled – students.

But when a powerful wizard is murdered with a misspell, Shannon and Nicodemus become the prime suspects. Proving their innocence becomes harder when the murderer begins killing male cacographers one by one, and all evidence suggests that Nicodemus will be next. Hunted by both investigators and a hidden killer, Shannon and Nicodemus must urgently discover the truth about the murders, the nature of magic and themselves. In doing so Nicodemus discovers that he is involved with a much larger story, one which could change the fate of his world, because not everyone interprets the prophecy in the same way. There are some who believe that he still holds great power and he becomes the target for this faction so they can bend him and his power to their will.

Nicodemus has importance as both a writer and interpreter of spells. In this world ensuring the correct use of language in the form of spells implies that spell books must be carefully guarded and their access monitored. Here word choice and sentence construction have direct consequences for the way the spells behave. Charlton imagines that magical language could behave like organic macromolecules: it would have the potential to fold into correct formation and so become effective. Because of this, Nicodemus's role as both creator and interpreter of spells becomes central to the survival of his world and the fulfilling of the prophecy.

The magical system in *Spellwright* depends entirely on magical languages and runes held in libraries of spell books. In itself this is nothing new, but Charlton takes the concept to a new level, one revolving around the system of writing, which is then governed by its own elaborate set of rules and theories and where familiar words like prose, literacy, edit, erase, censor, deconstruct, subtext, syntax, paragraphs and many more take on new meaning:

> As with any language, you will need to build a vocabulary and understand the grammar governing that vocabulary. After that, you will learn sentences, and finally how to cast them out into the world.
>
> *(Spellwright 2010, p. 101)*

This murder mystery presents an unorthodox view of dyslexia and chooses a cacographer as a central protagonist. Readers are invited to consider the power of words when confronted with the physical effort required to create them. They are also asked to evaluate what happens when the sense of the meaning is changed in a spell when the word order is compromised or the spelling is incorrect. Unlike the real world, in this secondary world the consequences of poor or careless spelling or unfortunate word transpositions have major ramifications.

Here the magical emphasis is on the power of language and the consequences of misspelling and misusing language within books. The play on language of 'spellwright' and 'misspell' is clearly deliberate at all times as is both the disempowering of the youthful cacographer – like his dyslexic creator – and the healing power of language. Nicodemus's harsh experiences both as a builder and receiver of misspells encourages ambivalent feelings about language and its intrinsic and extrinsic power. He transitions through seeing language as an enemy, then as a tool until his recognition of the power of language and its function as a means to an end forces him to review how he learns, reads and uses language to meet his needs. This in turn forces the reader to reflect on the potential power of words and of the effects of misusing them. And because this potential is personified in a hero – albeit a flawed one – who has a disabling and dangerous learning difficulty, the point is made strongly. In this book there is both language and magic sometimes pulled from books, at other times inserted into books. The attention that is focused on language and power challenges the reader to pay equal attention to both. Whether it is the language or the magic that is most powerful is perhaps left to the reader to decide but without doubt the interpretation of the language of spells is what provides the magical power that drives the plot in this challenging book.

Inkheart

The final book to be considered is Funke's *Inkheart*, an example of what Mendlesohn (2008) calls 'intrusion fantasy'; that is, a fantasy where characters from a book within the book emerge from their own story and interact with those from the primary narrative. It is the story of Meggie and her father Mo, a book repair specialist. They are both avid readers, and what distinguishes them from others is Mo's astonishing ability to read aloud: 'almost tenderly, as if every letter were a musical note and any words spoken without love were a discord in the melody' (*Inkheart* 2003, p. 279). It is this reading aloud which instigates the story – for the power of his reading is such that it animates the characters he reads about, not just in the minds of the listeners, but into the reality of their lives.

Meggie's mother disappeared when she was a baby but it is not until she is imprisoned by the sinister Capricorn that Meggie discovers her mother's true fate and her father's ability to read characters and objects out of books and into real life. Anything he reads into existence in this manner swaps places with a person or object that is nearby. On the night Mo discovered his talent extended to characters in books, he accidently read his wife into the book called 'Inkheart', while at the same time reading three book characters, Dustfinger, Capricorn and Basta, into real life. Dustfinger, a fire eater, desperately wants to return to the world of the fictional novel, whereas Capricorn, the villain of both the 'real' and 'imaginary' stories, wants to safeguard his own existence by destroying all copies of 'Inkheart' – the book in which he was originally a character. Meggie's discovery that she has inherited her father's special skill makes her both a target for the villainous Capricorn but also the potential saviour of her mother and many other characters in the book.

When Capricorn learns that Meggie has inherited her father's gift, he decides to have her read his favourite assassin, the Shadow, out of Inkheart so that he can make him execute Dustfinger and the maid Resa, who Meggie realises is actually her mother. Meggie and Fenoglio, the fictional Inkheart's author, turn the tables on Capricorn by altering the text Meggie will read. As she reads the revised words written by Fenoglio it is her intention to put an end to the villain Capricorn. Before it comes to that, even though she has begun reading, her father Mo intervenes and it is he who reads the words fatal to Capricorn. He does not want Meggie to have the death of even a fictitious character on her conscience.

On more than one level, *Inkheart* is a book about books and the love of reading: *Inkheart* references many other works of literature. In addition to the characters from the fictional novel Inkheart, Mo also brings to life a boy, Farid, who belongs in *One Thousand and One Nights*, and makes gold appear from *Treasure Island*. Meggie's reading causes Tinkerbell from *Peter Pan* to appear, and she also conjures up the soldier from *The Steadfast Tin Soldier*, a Hans Christian Andersen fairy tale, at the request of the Magpie, Capricorn's mother. Later, at the request of Fenoglio, she returns the soldier.

As is the case in many metafictive texts, *Inkheart* makes reading strange for both Meggie and the real reader. Young readers, particularly young adult readers, can be ambivalent about books and reading generally, though the fantasy genre seems to be maintaining or even gaining in popularity. That ambivalent attitude towards books and reading is given voice in this novel through the unfolding events as Meggie moves from the pleasure she derives from books in the early part of the tale where books are, 'friends that never quarrelled with her, clever powerful friends – daring and knowledgeable, tried and tested adventurers who … Cheered her up when she was sad' (*Inkheart* 2003, p. 15) and where the effect of the language of books is showcased by Mo's, and indeed Meggie's own, ability to read so that even the most hardbitten audience is enraptured and entranced. Her journey from almost wallowing in reading pleasure to a much more dispassionate and utilitarian use of the book may also be considered to mirror much of the experience of the young adult reader, *forced* to read in order to meet educational targets. But despite the trials Meggie encounters in this book, by the end of the novel her experiences have coalesced in such a way that she is determined to become an author in order to achieve, in her eyes, the ultimate form of agency. As an author she will decide the direction of the story, the development of the characters and the nature of the challenges she allows her characters to encounter.

The question of how stories within stories interlace to form an overarching structure and how characters function as both tellers of tales and readers assumes particular importance in metafictive books. *Inkheart* examines the intricate collaboration that is necessarily built up between tellers and listeners/readers of a story. By its nature as a metafictional text *Inkheart* underscores the distance between actuality and fiction, between nature and art. Readers are constantly reminded that they, like the characters they are reading about, are reading. When Mo reads characters out of a fictional text into the 'real' world, actual readers share the disruption of his expectations and this may result in a closer examination of how much as readers we 'buy in' to the worlds created for us in books. Such metafictional texts reveal challenges to expectations about child–adult relationships and especially in the case of Young Adult literature. This can be seen in Meggie's changing attitudes towards her father for having this almost magical skill for reading aloud and withholding it from her; for his seeming reluctance to recognise that she can handle complex issues and that she is capable of making her own judgements. Expectations about child–book relationships are also challenged in Meggie's changing ideas about authors and the authorial voice through her encounters with Fenoglio who sometimes can't remember what he wrote and clearly never considered the impact his words and stories might have on readers. Meggie's decision to be a writer indicates that she has wrestled with these challenges and has made her own peace with them allowing her to write from a more informed point of view and keeping her responsibilities to her reader towards the forefront of her thinking.

This novel features two characteristics that are often identified in books about books or reading: getting 'lost in a book' and writing – or in this case at times – re-writing a book. In responding to some of the incidents Meggie's reactions mirror those of the reader presenting encounters with fictional characters coming to life, played out within the story. This technique, far from distancing readers from the text, almost forces full engagement with it as readers are introduced to the consequences of interacting with written texts and the whole issue of animating characters. The fantasy genre of course allows this to be played out to maximum effect.

Funke creates an insular and word-driven world. For books like this to 'work' readers have to be already thoroughly 'book identified', because young people who read intrusion fantasies consume a model of slippages between fiction and reality that exemplifies a particularly engaged form of reading. Additionally, many of these books also depend on intertextuality recognised by the readers as well as having both passionate and reluctant readers in their cast of characters. A fictional character's emotional involvement with the characters from a novel can reflect our own reading experience. This is achieved through the self-reflexive, metafictive way these books constantly make the reader reflect on their own act of reading.

The idea that fiction affects reality raises the question of the responsibilities of the author and the reader of fantasy. The theme of the responsibility of the reader is dealt with throughout this book. We are shown the consequences of Meggie's reading when she releases characters from their original fictional 'homes' and when we consider the intention to deliberately use the words of the book and her skills as a reader to make the book into a weapon intent on destruction. Meggie's active reading has consequences for her and for the characters about whom she is reading. For the real reader the consequences are not so immediate but the impact of a book, of the author's words, can have a significant long-term effect as it works on the imagination and emotions of the reader.

The responsibility of the author is foregrounded as he or she is fundamental to the shaping and creating of the secondary world. But authors do not always change the story for the better – witness Fenoglio the author within the text and also Orpheus, from the second book in the series *Inkspell*, who uses his knowledge of the ways of changing Inkworld to his own advantage. Orpheus is a special case because he combines the powers of both author and reader in the same person. This reinforces the notion that characters are dependent on both author and reader. It is the combination of the powers of the author, the reader and the character which bring about the resolution of *Inkheart*.

Through her fantasy Funke causes us to reflect on our roles as readers and on writing and storytelling in general. We are made to take a step back from the text and our emotional involvement with the characters and actions. Thus, although the novels can be enjoyed without objective distancing adding to the meaning, they receive a wider significance through close reading of a second layer of interpretation which connects fantasy particularly tightly with reality.

Conclusion

The role played by books in each of these novels is utterly central to the narrative. *The Emerald Atlas* with the notion that individual characters make distinctive symbiotic connections with specific books; *Inkheart*'s transitory boundaries between the real world and the world of fiction; and *Spellwright*'s premise that words themselves have physical, moral and spiritual consequences and their accuracy, or lack of it, can have unforeseen repercussions present alternative views of how the book metaphor can portray magical aspects in fantasy fiction. In each book readers are invited to interrogate their own understanding and appreciation of the importance of language and of their own reading habits while at the same time allowing themselves to be submerged in the artifice the books and language demand within the tale.

Many fantasy tales involve a quest that requires the solution to a puzzle or a journey over hazardous ground. Many involve unlikely, and often young, heroes and heroines who are asked to make sense of a world with which they are completely unfamiliar or to undertake a task that seems totally beyond them. To do this they require knowledge, understanding and practical strategies – all of which can be provided by books and reading. Books are deceptive artefacts: books can be become keys and weapons if the language is understood and its power properly evaluated. Ursula Le Guin, one of the most influential writers of fantasy fiction has said, 'If one believes that words are acts, as I do, then one must hold writers responsible for what their words do' (1989). And this is perhaps why books and language so often feature as devices of potency and magic in fantasy fiction, weaving their spellbinding magic in the direction of both fictional and actual readers.

Primary sources

Charleton, Blake. *Spellwright*. London: HarperCollins, 2010.
Cooper, Susan. *The Dark is Rising* [1973]. London: Red Fox, 2010.
Cooper, Susan. *The Dark is Rising* sequence. London: Jonathan Cape/Chatto, 1965–1977.
Funke, Cornelia. *Inkheart*. New York: The Chicken House, 2003.
Funke, Cornelia. *Inkspell*. New York: The Chicken House, 2005.
Le Guin, Ursula. *The Wizard of Earthsea* [1968]. London: Puffin, 1973.
Levine, Gail Carson. *Ella Enchanted* [1997]. London: HarperCollins Children's Books, 2011.

McKinley, Robin. *Beauty* [1978]. London: David Fickling Books, 2011.

Nix, Garth. *The Old Kingdom* series. London: HarperTeen/HarperCollins, 1995–2014.

Sage, Angie. *Septimus Heap* series. London: Bloomsbury, 2005–2013.

Snicket, Lemony. *All the Wrong Questions* series. London: Little Brown Books for Young Readers, 2012–2014.

Stephens, John. *The Emerald Atlas*. London: Doubleday Childrens, 2011.

Secondary sources

Le Guin, Ursula. *Dancing at the Edge of the World: Thoughts on Words, Women, Places*. New York: Grove Press, 1989. Print.

Mendlesohn, Farah. *Rhetorics of Fantasy* Middletown, CT: Wesleyan University Press, 2008. Print.

Nelson, Claudia. 'Writing the Reader: The Literary Child in and Beyond the Book'. *Children's Literature Association Quarterly*, *31*(3), 222–238. 2006. Print.

Sanders, Joe Sutliff. 'The Critical Reader in Children's Metafiction'. *The Lion and the Unicorn*, *33*, 349–361. 2009. Print.

5

OF READERS AND VERMIN

The consequences of literacy for 'parasites'

Evelyn Arizpe

The life-changing consequences of literacy are often portrayed in children's literature and young adults. In some books, however, these consequences are not always the traditional benefits that one might predict and plots reflect how the path towards literacy is convoluted and fraught with difficulties. Given that 'literacy interrelates with the workings of power' (Gee 1996, p. 22), simply *wanting* to learn is often not enough when we are talking about characters who, because of their origins and/or social status, are expected by society – mainly, the establishment and the authorities – to be and to remain illiterate. A pivotal narrative device in many of these books involves the character who can't read coming into contact with a book or other text, such as in *Smith* by Leon Garfield (1968); *Lee Raven, Boy Thief* by Zizou Corder (2008) or *Holes* by Louis Sachar (2000 [1998]). In other books, such as *Trash* by Andy Mulligan (2010) and *The Baby and Fly Pie* by Melvin Burgess (1993), knowing how to read only seems to make matters worse for characters who are already struggling to survive.

Poverty and/or homelessness is the main cause of illiteracy in these books, so characters tend to be young teenagers who live on or off the street or on rubbish dumps, usually neglected and often abused by adults. Although these books are different in many ways, starting with the fact that they are set in different countries and/ or different historical periods (both past and future), there are several general similarities between them: first, the main characters are mostly all boys and they are orphaned or estranged in some way from their parents; second, they accidentally find or mistakenly steal something that does not belong in their normal, everyday circumstances: a wallet, a baby, a magic book. In the case of Smith and of Lee Raven, the objects are actually a document and a book which they cannot read. These objects act as triggers for the rest of the story because the teenagers are reluctant to return or give up the glimmer of hope they offer for the future. Because of this reluctance the characters suffer a variety of dangers: persecution, imprisonment and even torture.

These street children are often described as having rodent-like qualities: they are agile and streetwise and they can move almost invisibly through alleys or sewers. Because they prey upon and live off the establishment, mostly by stealing, they are also considered 'parasites', even though it is precisely because of the political, ideological and environmental structures of this establishment that they are construed as parasitical and threatening. Interestingly, in children's books, the majority of animals portrayed as readers are rats or mice and there is a striking parallel between books about literate rodents and books about street children. Not only are they both meant to be illiterate and unable to actually learn to read or write, they are also meant to be il-literary or non-literary, that is to say, their 'ignorance' is meant to go side by side with a lack of interest or ability to appreciate literature. As it turns out, some, especially the mice and rats, are even more literate and literary than most humans, whereas the characters who really are illiterate make up for this 'disability' by having imagination and creativity, by the desire to learn to read or at least, by having a fascination with words and stories (curiously, one of the metaphors used for obsessive readers is as scavengers, 'mice' in Spanish or 'rats' in German or French).

The characters' rather inexplicable attachment to a text or book is perhaps a reflection of some kind of intuition that these may be a ticket out of poverty, a way to an alternative future. This is certainly the case of the rats both in *Mrs Frisby and the Rats of NIMH* by Robert C. O'Brien (1975 [1971]) and in *The Amazing Maurice and his Educated Rodents* by Terry Pratchett (2002 [2001]). In cases, the rats and mice are able to in some way transform the lives of others, sometimes animals too but especially humans, as a result of their literacy skills, such as in the Miss Bianca series by Margery Sharp (1993 [1959]); *Walter* by Barbara Wersba (2005); *The Tale of Despereaux* by Katie DiCamillo (2004) and *Charlotte's Web* (2003 [1952]) and *Stuart Little* by E.B. White (1973 [1945]).

The illiterate as abject and parasitical

Human or animal, these characters are on the margins of society, looked down upon or even loathed by the establishment. In other words, they are considered 'vermin'. Christine Wilkie-Stibbs (2008) builds on Julia Kristeva's ideas on the abject in *Powers of Horror* (1982) to help understand the groups on the margins of society and her analysis of the 'outside' abject child can be applied to the street children and the rodents: 'Their bodies are excluded, rejected, extinguished, mistreated, or hidden; they are all conjectured in alterity and identified in the narratives as being in some way different ...' (Wilkie-Stibbs 2008, p. 81). Repulsive bodies and their fluids are very much present in these books: grime, sweat, blindness, corpses and rubbish, among others. The sewers and the rubbish dumps are places where rationality and meaning collapses; they are borderlands where roles are inverted and children are forced to be even more clever than the abusive adults around them in order to survive and, perhaps, escape from these hellish places (which they often share with rats). Literacy becomes one of these survival strategies.

Because literacy allows access to information and can lead to self-awareness and criticality in a Freirian sense (Freire 1972), it can also be a threat to the established order. The subversive power of the abject characters can be viewed through the theory of French philosopher Michel Serres (1982 [1980]) who considers that the relationship between humans and society is like that of the parasite and the host. The parasite disrupts systems of exchange so the host constantly attempts to expel the parasite but in doing so, positions can change. Serres identifies three types in this 'parasite logic': the parasites can 'analyse' (take but not give), paralyse (interrupt usual functioning) or catalyse (force the host to act differently). Through these actions, Serres argues, even unempowered minorities can bring diversity and complexity to human life and thought. This is applied to the relationship between society and authority and the 'parasitic' illiterate characters (who start off taking and/or are perceived as takers) as well as to the consequences (the disruption of the established order) that occur when these 'vermin' learn to read (the transformation of the system).

Most of the books mentioned in this chapter are intended for fluent, pre-adolescent or adolescent readers, in other words, readers who are (or should be) themselves literate. Therefore, the intention of the authors of books about illiterate children is not to encourage literacy (as might be the case in picturebooks intended for those on the verge of literacy) but perhaps to create a situation where the reader can imagine what it might be like to not be able to read. In the case of the books about rodents, the intention seems to be to prove that rodents who can read have qualities that put them on the par with humans; in other words, they stop being complete 'parasites' and give something in return or at least stop living off them. At the same time, they become, as in Pratchett's book, 'Changelings' or 'in-between' or 'ambiguous' creatures, another characteristic of the abject according to Kristeva. They are still regarded as outsiders and perhaps with even more horror: the escaped literate Rats of NIMH, for example, must be found and exterminated. However, whether they are concerned with humans or animals, these books lead the reader to question common assumptions about the links between marginalisation and literacy and, in some cases, to become more aware or critical of the circumstances that lead to their marginalisation.

The street and dump children: the power of language and cleanliness

Wilkie-Stibbs also uses Judith Butler's ideas on power and language to examine the 'outsider' child in children's fiction, and these help illuminate some characteristics of the illiterate subjects in these books, particularly to the children who have been expelled to the street or dump(ed). For Butler, 'the subordination of the subject takes place through language' (cited in Wilkie-Stibbs 2008, p. 90). Wilkie-Stibbs applies this idea to the lack of spoken language in characters that marks them as powerless, silenced and therefore a 'potential victim to be exploited, expunged, and exterminated' (2008, p. 91). According to Freire (1972), lack of access to the written word is also a form of oppression, with those in authority controlling both access to learning and to texts (a common theme in children's fiction, as can be seen in some of the chapters in this section). The ability to speak and to write one's name can be seen as the first act in the reassertion of the subject and this occurs in several of the books discussed here.

In Garfield's book, Smith does not seem to have a first name, he is only known as 'Smith' or 'Smut' – another reference to the dirt that seems to cling to him. Lee Raven uses a fake name, 'Joe English', and one of the characters in *Trash* is actually known as 'Rat'. Although Zero is not the protagonist of *Holes*, he falls into this category of illiterate street child and Wilkie-Stibbs also mentions him because, like other silenced abject characters, he is denied a proper name. It is not until he is able to read and write 'Zero' that he reveals his real name.

It follows that the lack of access to written language is also a metaphor for exclusion from the home, an exclusion that leads to exploitation, for example, by the adults who control the rubbish dumps. Lee runs away from home because he is physically abused by his father. Of all the street and dump children, Smith has the most agency; he has a home of sorts and his sisters care for him in their own way. Though he and the other illiterate children befriend a few kind people, for the most part the adults they meet consider them worthless and in some cases try to eliminate them, such as when Zero is described as 'nobody' by Mr Pendanski and the Warden orders all records of him destroyed thinking no one would notice.

The link between the children's bodies and the 'unclean' is a constant theme in these books. Although Kristeva says it is not lack of cleanliness that causes abjection, this link occurs because bodily fluids seem to 'cling' to them, and the spaces they are forced to inhabit – outside the system – simply add to this. The children are avoided and rejected because their surface appearance and the filth that covers them are perceived as an indication of disease. Lee Raven is 'dreadfully grubby' and becomes even more so as the story goes on, especially after he escapes his persecutors through the London sewers, wading through excrement, grease and slime (as it turns out he does contract a disease there known as 'rats piss disease'). Even death has avoided Smith, 'for fear of catching something' (p. 7) and dirt is almost a part of his body.

It is symbolic that Smith gets his first bath at the same time as he is about to be taught to read. It takes three hours to get him clean and he seems to lose part of himself in the process: 'he was taken out, rinsed, and wrapped in a sheet – the ghost of his former self' (p. 53). Clean clothes and body are associated with gentility and hence with learning to read. However, as the gaoler exclaims, his dirt hid a 'multitude o'sins' and now his cleanliness has, unwittingly, led to their exposure. Surface cleanliness, and thus learning, are considered no use when the 'sins' apparently go so deep, so much so that when he is thrown into Newgate after being accused of murder, Smith's fine new clothes are ripped and he rapidly becomes covered in grime again. Despite his innocence, it takes a long walk through heavy white snow and a near encounter with death to before he is 'cleansed' again.

Not all the street and dump children learn to read in the course of the story. Those who do, start with struggling to find someone who will teach them. Smith approaches a jailed debtor, a lawyer, a clerk, a schoolmaster, a bookseller and a priest. Not only do they advise him against learning ('Be happy that you can't!') because they believe he will not benefit by it but he is actually physically abused by some of them for asking. Ironically, as Smith himself notes, the only person who befriends him, the magistrate, can't teach him because he is blind. Rafael from *Trash* is a 'dump child' who has learned how to read at a mission school; he is a clever boy who can also use a computer. However, when Rafael is interrogated and tortured by the police, and they find out he can read, they exclaim, 'This piece of shit can read? ... Who taught trash to read?' (p. 62). The value of reading is denied to these 'nonsubjects' by the authorities who see this activity as a potential threat to the oppressive power of the system.

Along with lack of opportunity, there are other reasons for the children being illiterate but none has to do with lack of intelligence. Zero is brilliant at maths and picks up literacy quickly once someone has the patience to teach him. Lee Raven has been labelled as 'DYS LEX IC' which means 'STU PID PRAT' to his abusive dad. The letters 'dance around'; he 'can't make them out' so it all means nothing to him. He knows books are valuable but doesn't like them because 'they've got everything in them, and I can't get at it' (p. 11). He imagines that reading is like 'hearing someone else's words in your head' and is envious of all that can be gained by it. But of course he is not stupid, useless or even ignorant, and proudly claims, 'I can learn anything, anywhere, anytime' (p. 63). He also has useful skills such as picking pockets and locks as well as a memory map of the London sewers. The only book he remembers his mother reading is a copy of *The Beano* which he and his brothers loved to look at until his dad burnt it.

The book that Lee steals is a magic book that has the capacity to become which-ever book or story the reader most wants it to be (like the book in E.T.A. Hoffman's story 'The Choosing of the Bride', a kind of empathetic kindle). However, because Lee can't read, the book is forced to use its voice to tell him stories, and the first stories he tells him are from *The Beano*. The boy and the book develop a special relationship and become friends, so much so that even an enormous reward does not tempt Lee to return the book. He knows the book is something special and he feels the need to protect and care for it. Oddly enough the book is also looked after by a group of mice; they turn into dragons in one of the final scenes when the book transforms into a human figure, the god Nebo, the ancient Babylonian scribe god or patron of writing. When Lee rescues the nearly 'dead' book at the end of the story, there is a metafictional twist where it becomes the book in the hands of the reader, *Lee Raven, Boy Thief.* We don't find out if Lee Raven ever learns to read but with the book of Nebo as a companion it would be hardly necessary.

From the point of view of society and the establishment, these children all lead a 'parasitic' existence (sometimes they are hosts themselves as well, like Smith who is covered in lice which are scrubbed out of him during his bath). They take from others and give nothing valuable in return and 'interrupt usual functioning' by caus-ing trouble through acquiring money, objects and information that does not belong to them or by trying to learn to read. From the point of view of the characters, it could be argued that those who live on the rubbish dumps are simply taking what has already been discarded (and this kind of recycling also brings some benefits to society) and that stealing, as Lee ironically notes, can be regarded as 'performing a public service of redistributing wealth and preventing public drunkenness' (p. 2). It can also be argued that the trouble they cause by trying to learn to read reflects the fears of the disruption to the 'status quo' through the raising of awareness and the struggle for justice that literacy can lead to. Finally, it would seem that the authors of these books are suggesting that although these children are materially destitute, they do have a lot of intangible wealth to 'give', such as empathy, friendship and loyalty.

The mice and rats: disruption and civilisation

The books about mice and rats who learn to read or who use their literacy for a particular purpose are more heterogeneous. They all disrupt the established natural order in some way, but although they all also occupy a borderland, hybrid space between the animal and human worlds, these characters do so from a range of different positions according to which rodent or human-like qualities predominate. There is the sophisticated white mouse poet Miss Bianca; the avid readers, the rat Walter and the mouse Despereaux and the self-aware rats in Pratchett's and O'Brien's books; the latter in particular who are also highly literate. Although Stuart Little and Templeton can also read, Stuart Little is not entirely a rodent whereas Templeton is very much a rat; their literacy is taken for granted and is not the focus of the narratives; however, both are abject characters [Stuart Little's case has been discussed by Marah Gubar (2003), who equates his hybridity with that of the stage of adolescence] and Templeton does help to save Wilbur by bringing new words for Charlotte to weave.

In a sense, these characters are even more parasitic than the children, as they live off humans; however, in contrast to the street children, they all have a name and most of them are able to call a place 'home', whether it is a golden pagoda or a burrow, even if they are in the process of moving out or looking for a better one. Only Despereaux is rejected by his own kind for being different, not only physically but also for being more 'human-like' in his love for reading and for the princess. He is marched to the filthy, stinking dungeons to be killed by rats. Walter, the reading rat, lives in tolerant companionship with the owner of the house where he has his nest. There is a sense of community among the literate mice that form the Prisoners Aid Society in the Miss Bianca books and their solidarity, warmth and order are in sharp contrast to the cold, lonely and despairing atmospheres of the various prisons – whether they be dungeons, towers or the diamond Palace – from which they rescue unfortunate humans. The community of the rats of NIMH is clearly a metaphor for a particular kind of ideal society and both these rats and the 'Changelings' in Pratchett's books look after each other and work together.

All these characters retain rodent-like qualities to different degrees but there are often references to the fact that they are actually clean creatures who worry about dirt and disorder. When Miss Bianca and Bernard have to live in squalid conditions during their rescues, they do their best to be tidy and remain clean. Despite his forays into the drain and the trash, Gubar notes the frequency with which Stuart Little performs acts of hygiene (Gubar 2003). Walter the rat reader is tidier than Miss Pomeroy the human author. He grooms himself daily and is terribly upset by accusations that rats spread diseases as 'most of his relatives … had always been kind, clean and considerate' (2005, p. 9) and 'as far as he himself was concerned, Walter was a good rat – clean, neat, and thoughtful' (2005, p. 16). As in the case of the children, cleanliness is linked to literacy.

That the mice and rats in these books have somehow become literate is a focus for some of the narratives but in others this is just taken for granted. The Miss Bianca books are in some ways less interesting in terms of this topic because there is no explanation of how it happened (there is no mention of school but they are so organised that there must one). Miss Bianca presumably learnt to read alongside The Boy. However, the mice value reading and poetry, and it is texts that, in one way or another, underlie all their adventures. Despereaux inexplicably begins to read when he sees an open book for the first time and the marks somehow arrange themselves into letters and words. As a result, rather than eat the book he reads it, and this act releases a chain of consequences for himself and the rest of the characters. An innate ability to read also enables Walter to access books from the town dump and he reads his way through Miss Pomeroy's library. Of all the rodents, his is the most literary experience: 'Words swam through Walter's mind like bright fish, darting back and forth. He did not always understand what he was reading, but the experience excited him. All those images, all those thoughts and ideas!' (p. 10).

The rats and mice of NIMH are actually taught to read by humans as part of an experiment. The scientists start with 'shape recognition', and repetition of sounds and pictures of recognisable objects. As one of the rats explains later, at first they did not know what was going on because they did not know what reading 'was' (1975, p. 108) until one of the rats realises that he can 'read' a word on one of the lab signs. Reading helps them escape from the lab, but it is their stay in an empty house with a library that really changes their lives as it enables them to build an elaborate burrow that even includes a library and classroom and has electricity. However, it also leads to a split between the rats who are happy to live as rats (albeit with more comforts) and those who are worried about the fact that they did not have enough work to do 'because a thief's life is always based on somebody else's work' (1975, p. 147).

Some form of magic, absorbed when scavenging from a wizard's dump, is responsible for developing the intelligence of the group of rats in Pratchett's book. Although only one of them can read well enough to struggle through a book, the others can read enough to call themselves after the labels they find in the dump: 'Hamnpork', 'Nourishing', 'Darktan' and 'Peaches', among others. However, they have also become visually literate. They can read pictures in 'the Book', apparently a children's story about anthropomorphised animals ('Mr Bunnsy has an Adventure') and this leads them to try to wear clothes and adds to their philosophical discussions about animal and human nature. They can also read the pictorial language that Peaches invents in order to record a series of new 'rules' for rat behaviour. Like the rats of NIMH, the Changelings are unhappy with deceiving and thieving and these rules reflect their growing sense of morality and ethics. The only reason they have agreed to work with the unscrupulous Maurice is that they require money to fund a new rat civilisation.

One group of the NIMH rats also wants to create a more 'civilised' self-sustaining colony, through growing food and other hard work rather than 'stealing', as one of them says: 'We're just living on the edge of somebody else's [civilisation], like fleas on a dog's back. If the dog drowns, the fleas drown too' (1975, p. 150). Literacy has made these groups of rats conscious of their 'parasitic' nature and is also the tool they employ in their attempt to abandon this type of existence. The rats and mice in the other books also distance themselves from their natural instincts. Walter is also very self-conscious, although he takes food from Miss Pomeroy's kitchen, he is careful that he does not take more than he needs. Despereaux is more interested in music than in crumbs and Miss Bianca and her friends show how their literacy allows them to do something for humans in return for food and shelter.

Consequences and transformations

As the narrator of *The Tale of Despereaux* writes, 'Every action, reader, no matter how small, has a consequence' (2004, p. 117) and in all these books each act of reading, whether by children or rodents, has a consequence. These consequences are unexpected and sometimes even dangerous because those who perform this act, being 'vermin' and 'parasites', were not expected to be able to read in the first place. However, though the consequences do not always bring the traditional benefits that one might predict (and indeed not all of the characters become literate) in all cases, what is crucial is learning to appreciate what it means to read.

For the mice and rats, the consequences of literacy have to do mostly with altering the established relationship between humans and animal by befriending or outwitting them. Walter recovers his voice and is accepted as a friend by Miss Pomeroy and the rats of NIMH are able to save themselves and Mrs Frisby's family from extermination and perhaps escape to a less parasitical form of life. In some cases the established order is completely turned on its head, such as in the case of Despereaux, as he can now be friends with the princess and the light-loving rat Chiaroscuro can make free of the palace. Templeton has helped upset the farmyard logic and the pig Wilbur is saved from the human's axe. Miss Bianca and her friends outwit human jailors and rescue a poet and a little girl as well as previous jailor who turns over a new leaf and becomes the gardener of an orphanage. The Changelings negotiate living alongside humans and, in a surprising inversion of roles, demand wages for 'vermin control', in this case, cockroaches and other, 'non-literate' rats. From a cynical point of view, this consequence can be seen as literacy leading to becoming part of the 'status quo' that then oppresses others.

For the street or dump children, the consequences have to do with outwitting abusive adults and disrupting the authorities that permits this abuse to occur. Zero's ability to read Stanley Yelnat's name on the buried suitcase leads to the uncovering of the truth about Camp Greenlake and imprisonment of the abusive adults. In *Trash*, Rafael and Jun-Jun (who has dropped the nickname 'Rat') manage to escape the dump and the sadistic authorities and re-distribute the money stolen by the corrupt official. Lee Raven's loyalty to his friend the magic book leads to him and his brothers finally standing up to their violent father (and, although Lee does not learn to read, it is made clear that worse than being illiterate is being uncreative or unimaginative, as illustrated by the exploitative villain Nigella). Essentially, the books are saying that these boys are good and that it is through literacy that they have an opportunity to show this or to develop this quality despite their abject state.

Smith's encounter with the magistrate (who would ordinarily have been his victim) changes the boy's life, as it results in Smith having the opportunity to learn to read and advance in the world. However, Garfield writes that it is a 'strangely familiar feeling of pity' (p. 40) that makes Smith take the blind man by the hand and lead him home, perhaps making a point that underneath all his 'wickedness' this is a boy worthy of learning and it is telling that the first words Mr Mansfield uses to introduce Smith to his daughter is 'goodhearted child'. When victory in his 'battle' to learn is confirmed by Miss Mansfield, Smith's 'heart leaped almost to the skies' (1968, p. 66), a suggestion of both heavenly virtue and the elevated class status he aspires to and eventually achieve, yet it was not so much his new skill as his compassion that gets him there.

So the one underlying consequence of the act of reading that seems to be similar in all these books about abject subjects who become literate is that beneath the perceived layers of ignorance, delinquency, filth, rubbish or disease, these subjects are revealed as 'good', as defined by the traditional values of being kind, generous and noble, no matter what their previous 'crimes' – as defined by that establishment and those authorities – may have been. Literacy is linked to a cleanliness not necessarily of the body but of the soul, and hence the link to 'godliness'. Most importantly, as a consequence of becoming literate or 'literary', both their creativity and good nature are enhanced and thus they tend to change the course of their own and others' lives; in other words, it is through this innate 'goodness' of character that these initially marginalised and parasitic characters can sometimes alter or cause transformations in the very same society that rejected them to begin with.

Only one of the books discussed here deviates significantly in terms of the consequences of a 'dump child's' attempts to become literate: *The Baby and Fly Pie*. In this case, it is not the boy 'Fly Pie' but his sister Jane, who tries to teach herself to read in order to escape from poverty and virtual slavery. This is how Fly Pie introduces her to the reader:

> She was a good girl, you know the sort. While the rest of us were out having a good time, Jane would stay in and wash her clothes or do her hair. She was always trying to learn things – reading and writing or sewing or adding up.

She was stupid. Who needs to read and write on a rubbish tip? But she did it anyway and … she always turns out in a clean dress with her hair brushed and her good manners, even when she's had to walk through the dirt to get there.

(1993, p. 31)

In the end, none of Jane's attempts to be clean or 'good' or to learn to read is of any use. Circumstances force her to become a prostitute. She neither escapes nor changes the system, she is simply shot and her illiterate brother Fly Pie returns to life on the street. Without reading too much into the issue of gender in this case, this book is a reminder of the grim reality of thousands of non-fictional, homeless, illiterate children and the forces which work to keep them 'on the dump'.

Primary sources

Burgess, Melvin. *The Baby and Fly Pie*. London: Puffin Books, 1993.

Corder, Zizou. *Lee Raven, Boy Thief*. London: Puffin Books, 2008.

DiCamillo, Katie. *The Tale of Despereaux*. London: Walker Books, 2004.

Garfield, Leon. *Smith*. Harmondsworth, Middlesex: Puffin Books, 1968.

Mulligan, Andy. *Trash*. London: David Fickling Books, 2010.

O'Brien, Robert C. *Mrs Frisby and the Rats of NIMH* [1971]. Harmondsworth, Middlesex: Puffin Books, 1975.

Pratchett, Terry. *The Amazing Maurice and his Educated Rodents* [2001]. London: Corgi, 2002.

Sachar, Louis. *Holes* [1998]. London: Bloomsbury, 2000.

Sharp, Margery. *The Rescuers* [1959]. London: HarperCollins, 1993.

Wersba, Barbara. *Walter*. Honesdale, PA: Boyds Mills Press, 2005.

White, E. B. *Stuart Little* [1945]. London: William Collins, 1973.

White, E. B. *Charlotte's Web*. [1952]. Harmondsworth, Middlesex: Puffin Books, 2003.

Secondary sources

Freire, Paolo. *Pedagogy of the Oppressed*. Harmondsworth: Penguin, 1972. Print.

Gee, James P. *Social Linguistics and Literacies: Ideology in Discourses*. London: Routledge Falmer, 1996. Print.

Gubar, Marah. Species Trouble: The Abjection of Adolescence in E. B. White's Stuart Little. *The Lion and the Unicorn*, 27(1), 98–119. 2003. Print.

Kristeva, Julia. *Powers of Horror. An Essay on Abjection* (Transl. L. S. Roudiez). New York: Columbia University Press, 1982. Print.

Serres, Michel. *The Parasite* [1980; English translation 1982]. (Transl. L. R. Schehr). Baltimore, MD: The Johns Hopkins University Press, 1982. Print.

Wilkie-Stibbs, Christine. *The Outside Child: In and Out of the Book*. London: Routledge, 2008. Print.

6

THE FORBIDDEN WORD

Readers in dystopia

Vivienne Smith

Introduction: reader identity

I suppose it is inevitable that writers of books like readers. They have a vested interest in them. Without readers, we can say positively that the author is dead – or at least in reduced circumstances – for who else will buy their books?

And readers like readers in books. It is in them that they see their bookishness reflected and their values about reading upheld. Think of poor little Jane Eyre wrapped up in the curtain on the window seat with Bewick's *History of British Birds* on her knee. Who, reading the novel, does not recognise her comfort in text and seclusion? And think of John Reed, when he discovers her. The reader's outrage at his bullying is not just because of his treatment of Jane, but because of his boorish disregard of books and readerliness in general. We side with Jane as readers and as victims in a philistine world. We are horrified that he could *throw a book*!

This writerly ploy to engage the real reader with the fictional reader is not rare. We see it again in *Matilda* (1988), where our bookish heroine unites readers against her stupid parents and the tyrannical Miss Trunchball, and again in Margaret Mahy's wonderful *The Librarian and the Robbers* (1978). Miss Laburnum is the salvation of Salvation. She cures his friends of measles, brings him to stories and rescues him from the unimaginative arm of the law by filing him on her shelves in strict alphabetical order. (She is a librarian, after all.) Readers in the real world stand cheering at her side. How could we do otherwise? There is another example in Eva Ibbotson's *Journey to the River Sea* (2001). Here, the reader knows that Mia is going to be the right sort of protagonist when she spends the evening sitting on the ladder in the school library, furnishing her imagination with the wonder and excitement of the Amazon jungle. The reader knows too, that the governess, Miss Minton is sound. This is established early on by the anecdote about the umbrella, the boy and the puppy; it is confirmed when we discover that her heavy trunk is full of books. Mia's cousins, on the other hand, Beatrice and Gwendolyn, are unimaginative and spiteful. They would not save puppies and they hardly read at all. The message of all this is quite clear: readers (such as you and me) are good, kind, generous, resourceful, upstanding members of society. We fight for right. Indeed, we are right. Readers, quite clearly, are on the side of the angels.

It is flattery of course, but perhaps it is necessary flattery. Readers – especially young readers – need strong and positive images of readers and reading to confirm them in their understanding that reading is worthy behaviour, at times when peer pressure might suggest otherwise. It is partly from these images of reading that readers build reading identities, those constructs of self-image that sustain and fuel reading and reading choices. It is one's reading identity that determines if one reads, how much one reads, what one reads and what one does with that reading. Much has been written about how reading identity is formed in homes and classrooms and by society in general (Heath 1983; Chambers 2011; Gambrell 1996; Cremin *et al.* 2008) but there seems to have been very little written about the role of texts in this process. I want to suggest here that texts matter very much; that they are perhaps the most persuasive places for readers to learn about reading, about how other people read and, by extension, about what reading might come to mean to them. Further, I want to suggest that for pre-teens and teenagers, some of the best texts that enable that exploration of readers and reading are dystopian novels: those places where readers in the story have to read against the odds and against society, often in order to survive. Here more starkly than ever, are readers-in-the-story positioned as warriors of right. When this happens, the differences between Jane Eyre and John Reed transcend the domestic and interpersonal and become political. Reading becomes resistance: an act of integrity and defiance in the face of oppression.

The connection or rather the disconnection between reading and dystopia is well established in both literature and life. Political and religious leaders realised in the sixteenth century that the printing press made ideas available to the masses, and that rebellion against state and Church could be a consequence. In the twentieth century, as literacy became the norm, more than ever, oppressive regimes of all political persuasions proscribed texts, imprisoned writers, muffled the press and even burned books. This has long been reflected in literature, along with the idea that together with freedom of thought through reading comes individuality and the possibility of creative personhood. *Fahrenheit 451* (1953), for example, is as much about the discovery and maintaining of self as it is about oppression and book burning.

The novels I will discuss here are various. Some are set against real historical contexts. Others are placed in an imaginary time, often, but not always, the future. What they have in common is a child protagonist who, despite being deprived of text by a deliberate act of politics, maintains or develops a relationship with reading. What I want to explore here is how this 'reading against the odds' might be interpreted by the real reader, and what, by extrapolation, might be learned about reading as a result.

Felix and Tomas: children in war

War provides a particular type of dystopia. As well as the inevitable disruption and danger, there is a sense that war is an abnegation of what childhood should be. The Wordsworthian ideal of the free and innocent child in the countryside cannot be maintained in light of invasion, landmines and shootings. Two texts which explore war in terms of how it disrupts the innocence of childhood are Michael Morpurgo's *I Believe in Unicorns* (2005) and Morris Gleitzman's *Once* (2006 [2005]) (and subsequent titles). *I Believe in Unicorns* tells the story of eight year old Tomas. He lives, untroubled by anything, including literacy, in a small town in what seems to be one of the Balkan States. He is reluctant to read, so his parents send him every week to the town library to hear stories. An enchantress of a librarian, her wooden unicorn and the stories she tells win him for literacy. He thrives and becomes a reader. Then the town is bombarded and enemy tanks roll in. The library is hit and all is feared lost, but the townspeople rally. They save the books and the unicorn and store them in their own homes until the war is over and the library rebuilt. Peace finally comes, but it is only when the unicorn is restored to the new library that the reader feels that the world has been righted. The primacy of the word and of the imagination has been restored and all is safe.

What we have here are books, story and reading as value, as things that are worth saving *per se*, that persist and can be returned to. Through the hardship, uncertainty and sheer pragmatism of war, the imaginary world is cached safe: a promise of luxury in the better times to come when innocence is restored and imagination can be entertained. It survives in memory and as an act of faith. Like the image of the blackbird in R.S. Thomas's poem, *A Day in Autumn*, it is 'something to wear against the heart in the long cold'. Reading, the young reader learns, really is worthwhile.

For Felix Salinger too, in Gleitzman's *Once* quartet, story provides comfort. Felix, the child of Jewish booksellers in Nazi occupied Poland, has been hidden by his parents in a Catholic orphanage. When Nazi soldiers arrive to burn the convent library, Felix decides to run away and warn his parents. He takes with him just two things: the notebook in which he writes his own stories and his memories of Richmal Crompton's *William*. On the run and in hiding, Felix holds William and Richmal Crompton close to his heart. William is there in the stories he retells to amuse his friend Zelda and in the names the two of them take on as they assume new identities. Crompton is there – the one constant feature – in the naïve litany of saints that Felix recites to calm himself in times of crisis. Eventually, when Felix is forced into still deeper hiding, a copy of *William's Happy Days* is his sole reading matter.

What is it, then, that William *does* for Felix the reader? What is it in these very English, middle class pre-war texts that speak to the little Jewish runaway? Most immediately, and most convincingly, I think, is the emotional security they provide. For Felix knew William Brown before war disrupted his life: he had met him in the bedtime stories his parents read aloud to him. The William in Felix's memory secures a thread of continuity with the past and strengthens his link with his missing parents.

In this way, Felix's sense of identity is maintained. The stories attach him to the Felix he was and the Felix he wants to be again.

But any favourite text might have delivered this sort of emotional security. What is significant about William Brown is that he connects with Felix in other ways as well. For William's carefree life in the English Home Counties proceeds in curious counterpoint to Felix's fight for existence. Both boys, for example, spend much time in the woods: William and the Outlaws in perpetual and imaginative adventure with brigands and highway men; Felix, a real outlaw in terms of the Nazis, has to avoid sniper bullets. Both are fascinated by food: William's days are punctuated by birthday teas, cream buns and visits to the sweetshop; Felix, genuinely hungry for much of the time, fantasises about a whole carrot. Both spend time in barns: William and the Outlaws play, plot and argue in their old barn; Felix hides, cramped in a pit in Gabriek's barn for two long years. Besting figures of authority is a preoccupation for both. For William, authority means the irascible Farmer Jenks, Mr. Marks, his headmaster, and his sometimes stern father. He risks the loss of pocket money, the confiscation of various catapults, bows and arrows, trumpets and mouth organs and the occasional beating. For Felix, authority means German soldiers. He risks being shot dead or being sent to a death camp.

What William has, and what Felix lacks is safety from harm, the security of a predictable home life and the freedom to play. Felix's only access to these is through his reading, and that is what William provides for him: a vicarious childhood.

So what might the child reader of Gleitzman's books make of all this? Most clear, I think is the life enhancing effect that reading is shown to have. Reading (and remembering story) preserves Felix's sense of self-hood and maintains a playful core to this thinking that juxtaposes the political straightjacket of Nazism, and which celebrates naughtiness and forgiveness. What Felix knows, and what the real reader learns from him is that books are where better lives can be had.

But this is not all. Felix has one more use for Richmal Crompton. He uses her as a shibboleth, a test for liberal values. Felix knows he can trust Amon, the Hitler Youth boy, when he discovers they are both fans of William and, indeed, the bond the two boys develop though the books enables Amon to save Felix's life. Are we to believe that stories imbue the reader with liberal values and inoculates against fascism? I find this less convincing.

Demetria and Todd: children in future worlds

In some ways, Tomas and Felix were relatively fortunate in that they both grew up in environments where familiarity with books and stories was an expectation and a joy. They knew what books might be good for, and they could hold on to and use this knowledge, even when there were no books to read. Fictional children in science-fiction and dystopian novels do not always have this advantage. The two I want to explore here are Todd from Patrick Ness's *The Knife of Never Letting Go* (2008), the first of the *Chaos Walking* trilogy; and Demetria from Jan Mark's *Riding Tycho* (2005) and its sequel *Voyager* (2007).

First Todd: his inability to read is both a consequence of his upbringing and an engine of the plot of the trilogy. Todd is nearly thirteen; a boy on the verge of manhood. His home is Prentisstown, an isolated settlement on New World, founded some twenty years earlier by Christian settlers, looking for a purer, more simple life. They did not find it, and they live now in an all-male community. There are no girls and no women, but there is the Noise: the ability to hear each other's thinking, or, rather, the inability to stop others from hearing one's own thoughts. Mayor Prentiss, who governs Prentisstown, has caused all books to be burned and has discontinued school since the suicide of the teacher. Todd, therefore, has no books to learn to read with and there has been no-one to teach him to do more than simple (and still for Todd, inefficient) decoding. The consequence of this is not just illiteracy, but also ignorance. Todd and the other boys who are his contemporaries have only propaganda videos and the accepted narratives of the adults to help them make sense of the history of their settlement, and nothing to expand their ideas in any way beyond that. With no alternative discourses available, questioning the truth of Mayor Prentiss's authorised version of events is unimaginable. Todd and the others take on the lies of their society: the knowledge that the women died out through illness, that Prentisstown is the only settlement on the planet, and that anyone who leaves it dies. In this world, where thinking is transparent, there is no concept of deceit, and so Todd is confined physically as well as cognitively by his illiteracy. One who cannot imagine the possibility of life beyond the prison does not try to escape.

But despite the Noise, there is deception, and the boundaries of Todd's life are not as fixed as he supposes. When circumstances force his guardians, Ben and Cillian, to insist that he leaves Prentisstown, they give him a survival kit in a rucksack. There is food and first aid equipment. There is a hunting knife, and there are texts: a map to help him reach the next settlement and his mother's diary.

This is astonishing, and the significance of these texts is immediately obvious to both Todd and to the reader, for neither text ought to exist in Prentisstown. The diary should have been burned long ago: the fact that it has been saved reveals a deliberate and long term act of civil disobedience on Ben and Cillian's part. The map should not even be possible, because, as far as Todd knows, there is nowhere else to map. Its presence suggests something even more shocking to him: that there must be other settlements on New World. Together the map and the diary light a fuse of realisation in Todd's mind. Its spark exposes for the first time the layers of deception that have swathed his young life: the carapace of lies that Mayor Prentiss has built up around Prentisstown concerning its history and isolation and the secrets that Ben and Cillian have kept hidden, even from Todd himself. The fuse explodes the world he has taken for granted since childhood and blows away his confidence and his trust.

This confidence would have been fairly easily reconstructed if Todd had been able to read. The diary would have helped him reimagine his past, and the map would have enabled him to see a purposeful immediate future. But Todd, like the children discussed in Arizpe's chapter in this volume, cannot read. As so, for Todd the secrecy he has only just realised continues, and now the texts take on a duality: they become both holders of truth *for* him and withholders of it *from* him. They symbolise the knowledge which he knows he desperately needs, and his inability to access it. They are silent, yet full of the noise he needs to hear. They are of enormous worth and enormous frustration. They are an outward reminder of his ignorance, his help-lessness and his pride. For what thirteen year old boy can admit to a girl that he has been wrong about everything, or that he can't read?

Only when Todd trusts Viola enough to admit his difficulty in reading is he able to discover what the texts have to say. By then, the urgent message that Ben wrote on the map is no longer relevant, but the diary has a lot to teach. It tells Todd his mother's story, and through it he learns the true history of Prentisstown. But he learns more than facts, he learns about love and openness. The hope and the tenderness his mother communicates stands in sharp contrast to the hatred and violence of Mayor Prentiss and his advancing army. These qualities provide the solace and emotional security that Todd needs: they allow him to rebuild his under-standing of the past, rediscover selfhood and understand the present more clearly. The added factor is Viola. Because the text is mediated for Todd through her, those lessons in love and trust transfer. Sharing the text draws them closer together, strengthens their relationship and fortifies their resolve.

In the end, text in *The Knife of Never Letting Go* is an agent of companionship and healing. But it can only become so once it had been read, and this is why Viola is so important. She shows the reader in the real world that text, important though it is, is nothing without a reader to read it. The reader, far from being nerdy and isolated, is in fact, a figure of power and unity.

Like Todd, Demetria in Jan Mark's *Riding Tycho*, lives on a planet which has been settled from Earth, though she has not been told this, and like him, lack of text is one of the factors that locks her into a dystopian community. Her home is High Island, one of just two outcrops, remote and bleak, and far from the mainland. Low Island, the other, is a prison. Demetria lives with her mother and older brother, Bevis. They, and the other inhabitants of High Island – especially the women – live a life of utility and hardship. There is no luxury, no festivity, no music and no laughter. They have one annual celebration on Old Year's Day, and they celebrate with a funeral.

Demetria and Bevis go to school. There, Bevis and the boys learn woodwork and seamanship. These are the skills they will need as adults. Demetria and the girls knit. They learn to knit the garments that their mothers and grandmothers have knitted for generations to supplement family incomes. For some this means elabo-rately patterned jumpers. For others it means stockings. Demetria's family knits stockings. She has learned to read, and is better at reading than the teacher, but this is not an accomplishment that is valued. It is knitting that matters here, and she is mediocre at that.

In this community texts are few, and those few are functional and authoritative. The mail boat has long since stopped bringing anything other than official letters – such as the one Demetria's mother receives to say that a political prisoner is to be billeted in their shed. There are no newspapers or magazines, and the only books are the collections of disjointed sentences that teach children to read:

> *The great orne is a big fish.*
> *The sheep is a useful animal.*
> *A good girl learns to knit.*
> *What will happen to the bad girl?*
>   (Voyager 2007, p. 129)

Texts such as these admit no room for argument or questioning, and less still for imagination. This is reading to control.

Even story has been diminished and brutalised. Demetria knows that the function of story is to teach morality to small children, and it is a comfortless morality indeed. Of course she knows about the Little Mermaid, she who fell in love with a fisherman, and married him. And Demetria knows what happened next: the mermaid turned out to be a useless wife (she couldn't knit!), and so the fisherman bashed her brains out on a rock and gave her to the women, who made her into soup. Optimism, love and mercy are not features of Demetria's life.

And yet, this world of misogyny and brutality is a palimpsest. Beneath it, shadows of a richer, more imaginative consciousness can be glimpsed. The currents that carry logs and fish past High Island are called Tycho and Kepler, named after astronomers who looked into the night sky and wondered. The siren that wails when a prisoner escapes from Low Island is called the Banshee. How did this unimaginative community happen upon these names? As the story progresses, Demetria learns that she has been named after her own planet: Demeter. It takes a romantic imagination to call a planet after the goddess of natural bounty: it takes hope, love and generosity to wish that bounty on a child. What has happened to this hope and imagination? Even Bevis, Demetria's bullying brother has a name reminiscent of childhood play and adventure (see Hunt, this volume), though that play is tainted with misogyny. In her interaction with Ianto Morgan, Demetria begins to glimpse this richer alternative to life as she experiences it on High Island. Her story, therefore, is the story of hope rediscovered. While Todd learns of an alternative way of understanding the past, Demetria glimpses the possibility of a better future.

Riding Tycho is a text that is allusive and subtle. The reader who appreciates it will have necessarily developed reading habits that are imaginative, tentative and enquiring, qualities all of which have been quashed in Demetria and her contemporaries. Much of the power in the book is in the unstated contrast that is made in the reader's mind between her own, necessarily rich way with text and the deliberate misuse of it that is accepted as normal on High Island. The readers in the real world who see this are both delighted and appalled: delighted at the imaginative and enriching possibility of text and story in their own lives, and appalled at the possibility of its abuse. They learn not to take text for granted.

Mosca Mye: child in an imagined past

If dreariness is the key word for imaginative life on High Island, then exuberant superstition seems to characterise the Fractured Realm of Frances Hardinge's *Fly by Night* (2005). Here every day and some hours are named for one of the Beloved, the domestic saints who regulate daily life. There is Goodlady Cramflick, She Who Keeps the Vegetables of the Garden Crisp; Goodman Postrophe, He Who Defends Villages from the Wandering Dead; Goodman Palpitattle, He Who Keeps Flies out of Jams and Butterchurns; and hundreds more. Shrines are built for them, prayers and berries are offered to them, and babies, born on the days and hours of their festivals are named for them. So our heroine, born on the day of Goodman Palpitattle, is named Mosca, after a bluebottle.

Mosca is daughter to exiled scholar, Quillam Mye. They live, isolated from the rest of the village of Chough in bookish harmony, until Quillam dies. Then his books and papers are burned and Mosca is farmed out to the miller to keep accounts and read letters. She is useful, but not trusted, for, as everyone knows reading is dangerous. If you read the wrong books, the words crawl around your brain and send you mad. Mosca is the only person in the village, except the magistrate, who can read.

She is not happy. The village is awful. It is wet and dripping. Chalky deposits from the hills engulf everything, and she is bored. Starved of words and ideas and in danger of calcification of mind as well as body, she escapes with a delinquent goose called Saracen and Eponymous Clent, storyteller, poet, conman and spy. Their adventures in the troubled city of Mandelion are the substance of the novel.

Text, and who controls it, is at the heart of Mandelion's trouble. The villagers in Chough were right. Text is dangerous in this realm, though not in the way they imagine it. The Guild of Stationers has power of press and must sanction everything that is read. Only texts that bear the Guild's stamp are permitted. Thus there are chapbooks and ballads, and news bulletins. The public may be entertained and thrilled by text, but not encouraged to think. Reading texts, writing texts, printing texts that have not been passed by the Stationers is an act of treason. They seek to thwart opposition. Opposition comes in two forms: Radicals and Birdcatchers. The Radicals want fairer conditions for the poor and strive to achieve it through education. They run illegal ragged schools for poor children, and print revolutionary literature on their hidden press. They want to overthrow the Stationers. The Birdcatchers are priests and their followers from the old regime, whose reading of ancient sacred texts has prompted them to wish to free the people from the superstition of the Beloved, to a purer, higher ideal. They will stop at nothing, not even murder to achieve their aims. They strive to restore the monarchy and regain intellectual control of the city. For all three groups, text is seminal and secrets essential: their own are to be guarded and the others' uncovered. Intrigue, suspicion and betrayal, therefore, are inevitable.

Into the fray, come Mosca and Clent, partisan to none of it, but literate enough to cause trouble to all. They weave their way through this web of politics and power, pushed and pulled by opposing forces. Is Clent spying for the right paymaster?

Should Mosca pledge her allegiance to Pertellis the radical and join his floating school? Should she be persuaded by the eloquence of the Birdcatcher, Linden Kohlrabi, and his professed admiration of her father's words?

In this novel text leads and misleads, changes, challenges and manipulates. Clent wields words very often to his advantage, but sometimes he comes close to being destroyed by them. Blythe the highwayman is metamorphosed from thuggish robber to champion of the people, merely by the suggestive power of a poem. Mosca is enticed by words out of one life and cast into another more dangerous. She is swayed almost out of reason by rhetoric. Cakes learns to read and is released temporarily from her skivvying mind set; Partridge accidently encounters an illegal press and is murdered. Text empowers and text destroys.

In this novel words, both spoken and written, are powerful and unpredictable, riotous and unreliable. There are no safe messages here for the reader in the real world about texts as sources of comfort. Nor is there any suggestion that text will help the reader sort out the past or the future: it is too capricious for that. But words, and story, are rich and life enhancing. Mosca knows this. This is why, in the end, she chooses to live a life of adventure with Clent rather than accept the predictability and security of the ragged school. She chooses to live on her wits and her intelligence as her literacy has equipped her to do. The words Mosca imagines her father speaks towards the end of the novel as she drifts disconsolately on the river on a raft of rags might just as well have been addressed to the reader in the real world:

> "'If you want someone to tell you want to think,' the phantom answered briskly, without looking up, 'you will never be short of people willing to do so.' … 'Come now,' he said at last, 'you can hardly claim that I have left you ignorant. I taught you to read, did I not?' ".
>
> *(p. 415)*

Conclusion

Teaching children to read, as Quillam Mye did for Mosca is one thing. Teaching them how to be readers is quite another. I suggest that teaching anybody to see text as an instrument of power is something different again. The books discussed here, separately and together, show text in two ways. They show how text can be controlled by authority, and how, when this happens, individual and collective freedom is curtailed. This is both freedom to act and speak and, most important, freedom of the imagination. For, without stories, how can anyone see beyond the confines of their everyday world, and build the narratives that make challenge possible? Todd and Demetria make this point clearly. Both grow up impoverished as readers and as a result struggle to learn to read their worlds differently. Both find, eventually, through story, the courage to oppose. This does not make either of their lives safer or easier, but it gives them agency.

Mosca too finds reading dangerous. But she knows what words are good for, and so illustrates the other way that texts are used here. They sustain. For Mosca, words provide interest and excitement and possibility. They enable her to live life on the edge. For Tomas and Felix, it is a little different, but the basic function is the same: story, or at least the promise of story enables them to hang on to the people they know they should be and want to be again. Reading for all three of them, is about identity.

And so it is for young readers in the real world. They, just like Tomas and Mosca and Todd are continually in the process of constructing their own reading identities from texts as they read. Few of them, thankfully, have war and tyranny to contend with, but there are social pressures, some of which, for some young people make being a reader difficult. These texts, with their internally persuasive arguments about the power and importance of text, I suggest, give these young readers the courage to keep reading 'against the odds' in their own lives.

Primary sources

Bradbury, Ray. *Fahrenheit 451*. New York: Ballantine Books, 1953.

Brontë, Charlotte. *Jane Eyre*. London: Smith, Elder and Co, 1847.

Crompton, Richmal. *William's Happy Days*. London: George Newnes, 1930.

Dahl, Roald. *Matilda*. London: Jonathan Cape. 1988.

Gleitzman, Morris. *Once* [2005]. London: Puffin, 2006.

Hardinge, Frances. *Fly by Night*. London: Macmillan, 2005.

Ibbotson, Eva. *Journey to the River Sea*. London: Macmillan, 2001.

Mahy, Margaret. *The Great Piratical Rumbustification and The Librarian and the Robbers*. Boston: David R. Godine, 1978.

Mark, Jan. *Riding Tycho*. London: Macmillan, 2005.

Mark, Jan. *Voyager*. London: Macmillan, 2007.

Morpurgo, Michael. *I Believe in Unicorns*. London: Walker Books, 2005.

Ness, Patrick. *The Knife of Never Letting Go*. London: Walker, 2008.

Thomas, Ronald Stuart. 'A Day in Autumn,' in *Collected Poems, 1945–1990*. London: Weidenfeld and Nicolson, 2000.

Secondary sources

Chambers, Aidan. *Tell Me (Children, Reading and Talk) with the Reading Environment*. Stroud: Thimble Press. 2011. Print.

Cremin, Teresa; Mottram, Marylyn; Bearne, Eve and Goodwin, Prue. 'Exploring teachers' knowledge of children's literature'. *Cambridge Journal of Education*, 38(4), 449–64. 2008. Print.

Gambrell, Linda. 'Creating classroom cultures that foster reading motivation' *The Reading Teacher, 50* (1), September. 14–25. 1996. Print.

Heath, Shirley Brice. *Ways with Words: Language, Life and Work in Communities and Classrooms*. Cambridge: Cambridge University Press. 1983. Print.

7

READING AS PROTECTION AND ENLIGHTENMENT IN MARCUS ZUSAK'S *THE BOOK THIEF*

Jean Webb

In 1823, almost a hundred years before the advent of Adolf Hitler's regime which led to World War II, the German-Jewish poet, Heinrich Heine declared: 'Wherever they burn books they will also, in the end, burn human beings.' Twenty thousand books were burned in Berlin on 10 May 1933 in celebration of Hitler's birthday. The Nazis regarded the literature of the Jews as both a symbol and a threat. Joseph Goebbels, Reich Minister for Public Enlightenment and Propaganda speaking at the book burning of 10 May, incited the crowds to hatred of the Jews with the words:

> 'German men and women! The age of arrogant Jewish intellectualism is now at an end! ... You are doing the right thing at this midnight hour—to consign to the flames the unclean spirit of the past. This is a great, powerful, and symbolic act ...'.

The Holocaust (literally meaning 'death by fire') which ensued, saw the execution of six million Jews burned in the flames of the incinerators in the Death Camps during World War II.

The Nazis perceived literature as being dangerous to their desire for totalitarian rule and not without cause, for reading is a means of access to ideas, philosophy, thought, history and identity. It changes minds and shapes past, present and future. The best of literature disturbs and provokes the reader to think further and to pursue the labyrinths of the mind. Set in Germany in World War II, Marcus Zusak's *The Book Thief* (2005) is a thought-provoking novel which focuses upon the importance of books and reading as being central to humanity. Zusak brings together an exploration of the importance of reading and the subject of how the events in Germany prior to and during World War II could have been experienced by ordinary people.

The inspiration for Zusak's novel comes from the memories of his parents. They had grown up in Germany in the war years and then emigrated to Australia where Zusak was born and still lives in Sydney. As a child they told him stories of their experiences of the war. Zusak's experience of war-time Germany was therefore through story. Zusak notes:

> When I was growing up, I heard stories at home about Munich and Vienna in war-time, when my parents were children. Two stories my mother told affected me a lot. The first was about Munich being bombed, and how the sky was on fire, how everything was red. The second was about something else she saw.
>
> (Zusak, no date)

The second story Zusak's mother told him was about the treatment of Jews being marched to Dachau:

> One day, there was a terrible noise coming from the main street of town, and when she ran to see it, she saw that Jewish people were being marched to Dachau, the concentration camp. At the back of the line, there was an old man, totally emaciated, who couldn't keep up. When a teenage boy saw this, he ran inside and brought the man a piece of bread. The man fell to his knees and kissed the boy's ankles and thanked him ... Soon, a soldier noticed and walked over. He tore the bread from the man's hands and whipped him for taking it. Then he chased the boy and whipped him for giving him the bread in the first place. In one moment, there was great kindness and great cruelty, and I saw it as the perfect story of how humans are.
>
> (Zusak, no date)

Through his writing of The Book Thief Zusak's intention was to portray 'another side to Nazi Germany' which was to demonstrate that *humans are actually worthwhile* (italicised in the original). Initially he had thought of writing a biography; however, as a fiction writer he turned to the notion of a 'personal story about a girl' which he then coupled with his thoughts about a 'stealer of books' and the power of words, both those of Hitler and of his character, Liesel. What Zusak wanted to

> create was a character to juxtapose the way Hitler used words. She would be a stealer of books and a prolific reader. She, too, would occasionally use words to hurt, but she would understand their power to heal and give life through stories.
>
> (Zusak, no date)

In The Book Thief Zusak does not attempt to explain the acts of history but rather explores how people survived emotionally as well as physically helped by experiences associated with books and reading. The motifs of the power of words for evil and for good, the importance of books, reading and also music are wound together through this poignant novel acting against the physical atrocities ensuing from political incitement and violence. As a result *The Book Thief* is a very disturbing novel dealing with matters associated with war, childhood and the determination to survive. Paradoxically this story has a focus on death, who is brought to life as a narrator. Death overarches the text as narrator and as the pervading experience of those affected by war. The narrator Death points out that a focus is the survivors, 'the leftover humans' (Zusak 2005, p. 5). From the offset of the novel there is a raised consciousness of language. Death, as the narrator, takes the reader through Liesel's journey to emancipation. He adds his commentary and observations throughout with a raised consciousness of language by employing the technique of defamiliarisation. Words are dislocated from their normally accepted meanings thus making the reader observe life differently, as when Death talks about the sky at the moment when he will come for the reader at their moment of passing from this life:

> The question is, what colour will everything be at that moment when I come for you? What will the sky be saying?
>
> Personally, I like a chocolate-coloured sky. Dark, dark chocolate. People say it suits me. I do, however, try to enjoy every colour I see – the whole spectrum. A billion or so flavours, none of them quite the same, and a sky to slowly suck on.
>
> *(p. 4)*

Perception and expectation are disrupted and the reader is made aware of a conceptualisation of nature which is entwined with sensation and physicality. Furthermore Zusak's use of the literary technique of defamiliarisation or *ostranenie* reflects the state of mind and being of those who are caught up in war without understanding why or what is happening to them.

The Book Thief vividly takes the reader back to the pre-World War II period in Germany and situates Liesel, the protagonist, in the confusion of the growing tension. From the reader's perspective the context and time period of the novel are not specified at the beginning, for information which eventually places the action just prior to World War II is gradually introduced into the text. Guards are mentioned and there is a German phrase included in the dialogue (p. 17). This could therefore be either World War I or II however; the inclusion of a crashed airplane more strongly indicates war-time and Germany during World War II, although there were flying forces in World War I. The placing of the narrative in 1939 is not confirmed until twenty pages into the text, and this subtly emphasises a child's perspective of living in the moment and not in political time. Liesel is dreaming of Hitler 'listening contentedly to the torrent of words that was spilling from his mouth' (p. 20). Words become images and such powerful images are welded to emotions and into the subconscious, surfacing in dream and nightmare.

Zusak encapsulates the innocence of the child through Liesel's dream. Unknown to Liesel her family is one of the target groups of the Nazis as her father is a Communist, yet she is listening 'contentedly' to the dictator whose intent is to destroy her family and the child herself. The words themselves are what catch Liesel's fascination, not their meaning, nor the speaker, yet the power of the dictator invades even the depths of the mind of a child through the sound of his emotive speeches. The reader is thus positioned as a child with Liesel's confusions in the process of picking up clues and piecing together what is happening. Thus the twenty-first century reader and the girl in the book join together in trying to find out and understand what was happening in Nazi Germany at that time. Zusak employs a 'bottom-up' approach, akin to that employed in social history, to the recounting and development of understanding of the political and social history of the period. He places the reader in the immediacy of the experience of Liesel, who is caught up in the wider machinations of war. The perspective is an intensely personal one. The words of Hitler have been so pervasive that they have occupied her dreaming as well as her waking life. The reader is engaged emotionally and intellectually through the imaginative experience of dream following on into the actualities of Liesel's life. What Liesel learns is that the power of language can be employed for both evil and good, for subjection or for emancipation, but before she comes to such knowledge she undergoes a painful learning curve of suffering.

Liesel's story is punctuated by incidents of being left, beginning with the journey to the foster parents where her mother plans to leave her children to protect them, unbeknown to Liesel, from the growing animosity and violence from the Nazis towards Communists. On this journey Liesel's brother dies. At his burial an apprentice gravedigger drops a book which Liesel picks up. The subject matter of the book is a stroke of bitter irony as this will be the text which is her precious possession, her reading obsession: 'The Gravedigger's Handbook'. The 'Handbook' is also an echo of the fate of millions during the coming war and under National Socialist rule. Poignantly a child has the instructions for disposal of the carnage of conflict. Ironically Liesel is illiterate.

To learn to read is her obsession in Liesel's disturbed life. She sleeps badly and dreams of the trauma already visited upon her. Hans Hubermann, her foster-father, sits through the nights with the child 'as Liesel cried into his sleeves and breathed him in' (p. 38). Her obsession to learn to read consequently performs a dual purpose in that in addition to becoming literate the close relationship which Hans forms with her enables her to gradually come through the trauma. By his actions Hans teaches her, as Death observes, the meaning of a phrase 'not found in the dictionary' that is:

Not-leaving: an act of trust and love, often deciphered by children.

(p. 38)

Hans realises that she needs far more love and care as a traumatised and deeply distressed child. He also incorporates his own emotional experiences through music when he plays his accordion for her.

Liesel would sit up and hum. Her cold toes clenched with excitement. No-one had ever given her music before.

(p. 38)

Zusak's choice of the accordion for Hans's instrument is particular; he could, for instance, have been a guitarist which is also a highly portable and popular instrument, but the accordion, as Zusak emphasises, is an instrument which breathes, which has a musical language of its own.

The accordion's scratched yet shiny back exterior came back and forth as his arms squeezed the dusty bellows, making it suck in the air and throw it back out … . Papa made the accordion live.

(p. 39)

As an accordionist myself, I know there is a special relationship when playing the instrument of almost synchronising your breathing with the action of the bellows, like an external organ held close to the body. Playing an accordion is a physically embracing experience, for the instrument becomes an extension of the body which you almost hug to produce the sounds. Zusak's giving Hans an accordion raises further interesting connections with the potential for Hans's submerged character and also brings connections with political and subversive nuances from his past life.

Hans is sympathetic toward the plight of the Jews. As the story progresses Hans demonstrates courage in his subversive actions by, for example, continuing to carry on his business as a decorator while he can, irrespective of whether or not his clients are Jewish. A further act of humanity and courage shared with his wife is that of sheltering a Jew in the basement of their home. Here the connection is made with his accordion. Hans was taught to play the accordion in World War I by Erik who was the father of Max Vandenburg, the very Jew he will later hide in his basement. Hans had salvaged the accordion from the rubble surrounding Erik's shell shattered body. The instrument thus holds layers of memory and association beyond the immediacy of the music itself. One can also conjecture that the tunes and melodies which Hans learned from his Jewish friend would not necessarily have been German folk and popular tunes, but those from the Jewish tradition, adding a further layer of subversion surrounding the seemingly innocuous act of playing the accordion. At home his playing at breakfast also incenses his wife, which also called for some 'courage'! For Liesel the sound of the accordion was 'in actual fact, also the announcement of safety' (p. 39).

There is further significance in Zusak having made Hans an accordionist, for historically the accordion had very strong associations with German national identity. Invented in Germany by Christian Friedrich Buschmann in 1822, the piano accordion was developed and patented by Cyrillus Damian in 1829. As a very portable instrument it was taken abroad by German emigrants when they left to escape the poverty of nineteenth century Germany. Between 1841 and 1913 more than six million Germans emigrated, many of them to America. The popularity of the accordion was marked by requests for instruments to be sent to the American set-tlements and also by sales representatives setting up business in America. Although it remained popular as an instrument with the German public, it was not beloved by the Third Reich. They strongly objected to classical music being played upon the accordion as it was thought to 'pollute' the purity of music which embodied the Germanic spirit. Furthermore the accordion was associated by the Nazis with the jazz and rhythms of African American music which had been taken up by German emigrants during their time in America and the instrument was therefore further objected to on racist grounds. When the Nazis came to power the manufac-ture of accordions slowed. Hans as an accordionist therefore takes on subtle political and humanitarian nuances.

The accordion music creates an emotional bond between Hans and Liesel in addition to his looking after her. It is a natural progression for Liesel to accept help from Hans to learn to read when they realise that she is significantly way behind the other children in school. The act of learning to read brings together the traumatised child and her somewhat awkward, hen-pecked foster father: security and love are founded through the process of learning to read and being read to. The subject matter is almost immaterial: the book as an object is important as this is a material link with her painful history. For the only book in the Hubermann household (p. 39) is 'The Gravedigger's Handbook' which Liesel picked up and now sleeps upon under her pillow even though she cannot read it (at first). As Death points out,

> It didn't really matter what that book was about. It was what it meant that was more important. [For Death knows that to Liesel]
>
> THE BOOK'S MEANING
>
> 1. The last time she saw her brother.
> 2. The last time she saw her mother.
>
> *(p. 39)*

Liesel's learning to read, becoming part of the Hubermann family and being settled with them means that she also has to take part in the activities expected of a ten year old child in Germany at that time, which included joining the Bund Deutscher Mädchen, the United German Girls, which was part of the Hitler Youth Movement. This was obligatory as part of the socialisation process required by the Third Reich to ensure a compliant generation to further their future political and social aims. There is no option but to conform, although Hans and Liesel are neither enthusi-astic nor convinced about the activities as indicated by the fact that they 'never spoke about it much. They just held hands and listened to their feet' (p. 41). Again Zusak conveys the depth of feeling and thought by unconventional use of language. The silent resistance of Hans and Liesel is symbolised in that they focus on their own bodies and listen not to the words of power circulating about them, but their own feet. This action is invisible to the outside world and seemingly insignificant but demonstrates the way in which Hans and Liesel create a barrier to the language of the symbolic order of the politically and ideologically dominant. Their subversive acts are quiet and personal and show how one could imagine that the ordinary people who were not swayed by Fascist views might have protected themselves from the ideology and propagandist fervour in pre-war Germany.

Liesel's fascination and obsession with books takes her into other areas of the impact of war when she steals books from Helena Schmidt, the mayor's wife, one of her foster-mother Rosa's customers, as Rosa does ironing and laundry to make money for her family. Frau Schmidt is lonely and depressed: wealthy, but unhappy. Her only son was killed fighting in World War I and since then she has been withdrawn and deeply lonely. She is described as having 'the posture of defeat' (p. 44); she has been broken by her bereavement resulting from the 1914–18 war which continues to have repercussions in her life. Fortunately for Liesel, Frau Schmidt has a rich library of books from which Liesel steals. Liesel's initiation into the conventions of libraries is somewhat unconventional, however, her breaking conventions also leads to the breaking down of emotional boundaries as a bond is gradually formed between the old woman and the child. Books and reading are the catalysts. The written words of others enable these traumatised people to speak to each other and to overcome some of their deep loneliness.

In *The Book Thief* literature and reading is a liberation for some whilst being a threat to others. A consequence of literacy is in one way freedom, in another, persecution for those who wrote 'un-German' books. Zusak takes the reader into the heart of the tension and hatred which consumed Germany during those years leading up to World War II, symbolised by the book burning ceremonies one of which was referred to above. The context which underpins Liesel snatching the second book which she owns is the Nazi booking burning of 'un-German' books.

> On April 6, 1933, the German Students Association's Main Office for Press and Propaganda proclaimed a nationwide 'Action against the Un-German Spirit,' to climax in a literary purge or 'cleansing' (*Säuberung*) by fire. Local chapters were to supply the press with releases and commissioned articles, sponsor well-known Nazi figures to speak at public gatherings, and negotiate for radio broadcast time.
>
> On May 10, 1933, in a symbolic act of ominous significance, the students burned upwards of 25,000 volumes of 'un-German' books, presaging an era of state censorship and control of culture. That night, in most university towns, right-wing students marched in torchlight parades 'against the un-German spirit.'
>
> *(United States Holocaust Museum)*

Liesel has first-hand experience of the translation of propaganda and incitement to violence and action when Max Vandenburg, a Jew, hounded and persecuted by the Nazis is given shelter by Hans and his wife in 1940. The action in Germany had deepened into the pursuit and murder of Jews. As Hans feels about his accordion, so Liesel feels about her books, including the ones which Hans has procured by trading cigarettes. The only way in which Hans can think to enforce the seriousness of the situation should she tell anyone about Max being hidden in their home is to threaten to burn her books if she disobeys the order of silence.

The importance of literature is continued through Max, the Jew confined for his safety to the basement rooms. To pass the time Max writes his own book. In an act of defiance and black humour he paints out and overwrites a copy of Hitler's *Mein Kampf*, writing of his own life and struggles, blotting out those of his persecutor and the persecutor of his race. Books by Jews had been forbidden and Liesel is the reader of one such book: a statement of defiance and refusal to be downtrodden by both Max and his young reader Liesel. There are multiple paradoxes here. Firstly, as Max says, *Mein Kampf* was the book which saved his life, despite the content, for hidden inside the book on a loose leaf was the map to the Hubermann household. It had also become obligatory for people to own and carry a copy to overtly display their 'loyalty' to Hitler and the Nazi Party, whether it was true or not. The title of *Mein Kampf* ('My Struggle') also ironically encapsulates the life of Max, for his very existence has been a struggle against political and religious oppression and the eradication of his race. Finally and in the greatest intellectual act of subversion before he has to leave the safety of the Hubermann's, Max inscribes his life over that of Hitler so that only the biography and struggles of a Jew can be read.

As she grows older writing also comes to be as important a personal act for Liesel as reading. On being given a blank book she takes control of her own narrative and writes her own life story which she calls 'The Book Thief'. The powerless become powerful through words, through language, through the courage to record that which is both the source of pain and of enlightenment. Being read to by Hans was solace, relief from the torturous experiences which were already embedded in her short life. Reading in the library was escape and comfort: finding new places albeit in the imagination. Witnessing Max write his book, blanking out the words of Hitler and replacing them with the words of an imprisoned Jew was witnessing an act of empowerment. His words disempower the words of the persecutor of his race and Liesel's enemy. Liesel's own book, her life story, is empowering. By recording her story she is also growing to understand, to gain knowledge about her own circumstances and experiences; starting to control the past, to control the trauma. The very act of writing in the basement saved her life, because the house was bombed and all her loved ones were killed while they slept in the upper rooms. In despair Liesel drops her book and it is retrieved by Death who reflects:

> After that, there were weeks and months, and a lot of war. She remembered her books in the moments of worst sorrow, especially the ones that were made for her and the one that saved her life. One morning, in a renewed state of shock, she even walked back down to Himmel Street to find them, but nothing was left. There was no recovery from what had happened. That would take decades. It would take a long life.
>
> (p. 550)

What is left though is Liesel's text, the record of her memories and fears, emotions and events, held safe by Death who returns the book to her when he comes to collect her in her old age and she can hold those deep memories through her own narrative when:

> The fingers of her soul touched the story that was written so long ago in her Himmel Street basement.
>
> *(p. 553)*

Death had read her story many times and in death her story retains life and nurtures hope. *The Book Thief* is far more than escapism as fiction can popularly be viewed; it is testament to reading as a form of protection and a force for enlightenment and reason when contemplating the awful confusions of human actions both past and present. Perhaps *The Book Thief* has stolen a little hope from the desolation of the ravages of a dreadful abomination upon human history … .

Primary sources

Zusak, Markus. *The Book Thief.* London: Doubleday, 2005.

Secondary sources

Goebbels, Joseph (1933) "German men and women …". Available at http://www.ushmm. org/exhibition/book-burning/burning.php (accessed 5/2/2015). Online.

Heine, Heinrich (1823) "Wherever they burn books …". Available at http://www.brainy-quote.com/quotes/quotes/h/heinrichhe104489.html#ELBukBmGpz17rzv9.99 (accessed 5/2/2015). Online.

United States Holocaust Museum (no date). Available from http://www.ushmm.org/exhibition/book-burning/burning.php (accessed at 19/5/2015). Online.

Zusak, M. (no date) *Markus Zusak talks about the writing of The Book Thief.* Available at http://www.panmacmillan.com.au/resources/MZ-TheBookThief.pdf (accessed 5/2/2015). Online.

PART III

Reading in new ways

Who is in control?

8

READERS' PERCEPTIONS OF A WRITER

Jacqueline Wilson's *persona* and her relationship with her readers

Julia Eccleshare

Children as readers are changing; the image of the solitary 'bookworm' child lost in the private world of a book has been replaced by a perception of reading as a social and collective activity. It's a positive step for reading as it implies that reading habits reflect the trends of shared responses that are at the core of twenty-first century media. Part of the change is reflected in the desire of children to be reading the same book as everyone else; hence, the increasingly narrow choice of authors named on lists of favourite readers. Another part of it is that children have begun to see the author or illustrator as a vital part of the 'story' they are enjoying. The result is the relationship between children and the authors that write for them has changed. As both a best-selling author and highly visible one, too, Jacqueline Wilson has played a significant role in the changes to the way children's books are currently being discovered and enjoyed.

The first relationship and connection between the writer and the reader lies in the words that link the two. After the invention of the printing press replaced the storytelling traditions which enabled the author to change texts to suit their particular audience and to embellish stories by performance, the writer's work became fixed. For many readers, therefore, the writer of the book was of little importance. The author's name and the small biography that the book might carry about them on the flyleaf was as much as most readers knew about the creator of the story they had enjoyed and, with few ways of finding out more, they rarely delved for further knowledge. In the absence of extensive arts or cultural journalism and few readers of them when they did exist, writers were known to readers through their books alone; they delighted their readers with the stories they told and built up their audiences on that basis.

Though the story remains the primary link between the writer and the reader, the way that link is fashioned is no longer as fixed as it was. Changes in the market place over centuries and, more recently, in the technology of book production, book selling and book reading are altering books as physical objects and how they are read. With the growth of consumer technology, what a 'book' now is and therefore how the story is 'read' is altering all the time. The two most obvious changes are in the development of audio books and ebooks. On the one hand, children's enjoyment of stories through audio books took a long time to be accepted as a valid alternative form of reading; ebooks, on the other, which it was thought would be of particular appeal to children have proved, thus far, to be considerably less popular than anticipated.

In terms of a market place, changes in the way books are discovered and bought, in particular on-line, have made books available outside the confines of specialist bookshops. Traditionally for book buying families, and especially in children's books, knowledgeable booksellers have helped readers to choose the books that they thought they would like. For individual children who were known to their local bookseller and were therefore able to have books hand-selected for them this was a highly successful way of being introduced to favourite authors and to sharing the most up to date information about trends in reading. With fewer such specialist shops in existence this kind of guidance – never widespread – is less common.

Now, with the possibility of buying any book on line at any time, the carefully 'managed' space which promoted particular books to particular readers has been superseded by a far larger but unselected array of titles. To navigate this uncharted wealth of material is difficult; finding a new book is hard unless potential readers already know the title and author of the book they are looking for.

To support this changing picture of buying opportunities various information sources – both web and print based – have attempted to offer advice and linked recommendations. Discovery of titles has also been provided by book lovers of all kinds – committed parents, knowledgeable librarians and, perhaps most usefully, through peer-to-peer advice on sites such as Cool Reads (http://www.coolreads. co.uk/), which was founded as its young initiators grew up. And books of carefully selected 'choices' such as Daniel Hahn et al.'s *The Ultimate Book Guide* and *Great Books to Read Aloud*, one of Jacqueline Wilson's Children's Laureate projects, highlighted some of the best books for that specific purpose.

Alongside the specialist bookshops, for children as readers, the library has traditionally played a significant role in helping to put the right book into the right hands. Anecdotally, and author Anne Fine is eloquent about this, many recall the role a librarian – or just the carefully catalogued books on tempting display in the library – played in helping them to become readers. But libraries are less used and, like the bookshops, are changing rapidly with the rise of new technology. Increasingly they are developing themselves as information centres more focused on learning opportunities than the traditional bedrock of resourcing reading for pleasure. The changes to these two key discovery sources may not look as if they would influence the relationship between the reader and the book, but they are significant in their impact on how any reader may now find an author. And on how any author may find a reader.

Coincidentally with this decline in informed, professional-led guidance and the role of the external mediator between child and book, the profile, status and job of children's writers in the publishing and selling of children's books altered significantly. Factors for this transformation were founded on the changing possibilities of children's books which were shaped by many factors and totally transformed by the response to J. K. Rowling in the years following the publication of *Harry Potter and the Philosopher's Stone* in 1997.

The changing role of authors was not an isolated cultural event. In the latter half of the twentieth and early part of the twenty-first century, across all the arts, the secret artifices of creativity have been deliberately demystified and the protected spaces around them have been replaced by an emphasis on accessibility, often underpinned by the deconstruction and questioning of post modernism. In the visual arts, the 'art' is explained by those who create it and the accompanying film of an artist at work is often as important as the exhibition itself. Understanding the inspiration for abstract art and particularly for installations is not left to the imagination of those who view. Instead, it is made public as part of the artwork itself. In a similar way, for readers, the increased focus on author interviews which reveal working environments, writing rituals and the supportive talismanic objects that inspire their creativity is designed to enable readers to understand more.

For children as readers a further step has been taken: meeting the author is seen as the key to unlocking the story and to providing the readers with insights which will enable them to enjoy it more. To have asked, "Where do your ideas come from?" implies an intimacy and complicity with the author which appears to demystify reading – not just the book in question or the author's work more widely, but reading in general.

The impact of this media-wide shift in cultural engagement has been accelerated in the past two decades by the concurrent rise in all areas of the celebration of the celebrity and the space that those who are well-known are given in the media. The author is now a 'celebrity' at least within the book world and often beyond too. Authors become household names and even 'brands'. They appear in places other than book jackets and even in other media. They are co-opted to fight for good causes – as Philip Pullman was for the campaign against the closure of the boatyard in Oxford. More glamorously, when books are turned into films or plays, they walk the red carpet and they rub shoulders with performers.

But even in a school setting where there is no additional glamour, evidence shows that the impact on meeting an author has increased reading for pleasure. 'Knowing' an author or even just seeing that an author is a living person changes young readers' view of books. Books are no longer perceived as static and passive and therefore old-fashioned; they are not the property of adults who 'select' them for arcane reasons. They are instead injected with whatever energy or personality the author brings to a live event. The author becomes part of the story; the characters and their actions are 'related' to them – frequently are even thought to be them – and so become no longer wholly imaginary and fanciful.

It is not just the public presence of authors that has impacted on children's access to stories and reading. Even for pre-school, or perhaps particularly for pre-school children, the story in its book form is rarely a single or specific entity. It is just as likely to be part of a multi-media cultural offer supported by additional merchandising of all kinds, most of which is character led. As with the extra dimension brought by the presence of an author, so the soft toy Elmer for those who enjoy David McKee's stories about the eponymous patchwork elephant, or the cuddly plush puppy Spot for readers of Eric Hill's *Where's Spot?* and its sequels make a tangible link to the book. These examples of 'additionality' play a part in shifting books from the private space to a more public one; 'playing' with Spot is an interactive or social way of engaging with the more static book.

Where previously their work spoke for the writers, the writers now speak for it themselves; 'knowing' the foibles and unusual details of an author's life is seen to add enjoyment. At its simplest, to help make the writer an ally or co-conspirator in the reading of the book, the once-straight author biographies at the front of books were transformed into the now familiar and often tiresomely trivial accounts which have been specifically designed to make the author seem 'fun'. Lists of pets or unusual jobs – putting the jam into a doughnut is one example – are designed to evoke a 'childlike' or at least an un-authoritarian persona for the author which will make the book more approachable. More recently, authors have spent much energy in making their websites rich resources of information, typically presented in humorous and eye-catching ways to increase a sense of author personality, even though, in reality, these bring only a small amount to bear on their books.

These developments have also brought about a shift in the perception of children as readers and the ways in which they can be reached. Instead of being treated as passive, silent and individual they are regarded as active, noisy and above all collective participants. The very private activity of reading has been changed – many feel enhanced – by the communal experience of meeting an author and 'sharing' delight in them and what they have to say with other readers.

At first this process was gradual; some authors were able to meet their readers and engage with them, others could not. Now, part of an agent or publisher's consideration when taking on a new author is: can they talk? How will they do in public? With libraries in decline and the big bookselling chains stocking a decreasing number of titles, children's authors are now making their own markets by speaking to children in schools and at book festivals.

Once the mystique of the writer as a remote and unknown being, except in the somewhat arid form of author studies, had been broken down and the market for meeting them had been given an uplift by the celebrity status of Rowling and some others, meeting writers became a useful tool in the reading for pleasure component of the teaching of literacy.

The opportunity for a more ambassadorial role came coincidentally with the National Literacy Strategy. The NLS took a fresh look at the teaching of reading and levels of literacy in primary schools. Shocked at what it found, it determined to create a 'literate' nation by imposing a highly structured, word-level approach to literacy. Though there was little scope within the basic framework for writers (or even whole books) there was a less publicised but far more valuable directive that both children and teachers should read 'modern fiction by significant children's authors'. Apparently an obvious and unremarkable proposal, it gave a push to the books by contemporary writers which could be furthered and built on by their actual appearance in a school.

Here was an important new role for writers who could now be invited not only to enthuse children as readers but also to be used as the spur to 'creativity'. Teachers needed this as, in the target-driven culture of the NLS, they became nervous of spending time in this way. Authors, just by being the physical embodiment of creativity in general and then specifically by answering questions about how they write, where they get their ideas from, when they wrote their first book and more, became much more common both in classroom visits and in the rapidly expanding new business of literary festivals.

The importance of reading on writing and the role of the writers themselves in it was first channelled in schemes such as Writing Together (BookTrust) and Everybody Writes (BookTrust) and then researched in studies such as Sue Horner's *Magic Dust That Lasts* (2010) – a national report on the impact of writers' residences in schools for Arts Council London.

And it wasn't just in the classroom that the profile and role of children's writers were changing. As is fitting in a society which likes to create stars in every field, a small handful of writers have become celebrities which further enhanced their role and influence. In tune with all other successful 'products', authors became the 'brand'. This has mostly applied to the very big sellers such as J. K. Rowling, Anthony Horowitz, Eoin Colfer, Christopher Paolini, Michael Morpurgo, Cressida Cowell, Robert Muchamore, Julia Donaldson and Jacqueline Wilson. These authors have become used to being treated as 'stars' and, in particular, to being mobbed at festivals where the chance of getting a book signed has turned children into a nation of queue-formers.

Traditionally, in children's literature when 'writers' are described – which is not often – their way of working is shown as solitary. Mother, in E. Nesbit's *The Railway Children*, works at home. She is mostly quietly shut away doing her writing. Her children know about her success not because she dashes off to Edinburgh, Hay or Cheltenham to speak to her readers but because there are buns for tea when she sells a story. Now, the role of the author is described very differently by children's writers. Marcus Sedgwick, himself a tireless visitor to schools at home and abroad and performer at literary festivals and teachers' conferences gives a telling and somewhat chilling insight into the life of a contemporary writer in his recent novel *She is Not Invisible* (2013). Within the exciting adventure which leads his children on a desperate trip to New York to find him after he disappears, the Dad of the story is a writer. He is not a writer of children's fiction but his experience fits nonetheless and many writers of all kinds would identify with his predicament; he was once very successful with a kind of book he no longer wants to write. Although Dad's life as a writer is not the main purpose of the book, Sedgwick gives many tell-tale glimpses into how authors' time may currently be used: Dad has many readers and receives much fan mail. Of course he is delighted but he also sighs "But I'm just so busy at the moment ...". His daughter is already paid a small fee to deal with his mail; Dad is flown to New York because he is up for an award and needs to attend the dinner in Manhattan. The publishers send a limo to fetch him from the airport. It all sounds like the high life which could be every author's dream. But is it?

Jacqueline Wilson presents an even darker picture of the life of a writer in her historical novel *Opal Plumstead* (2014). The one hopeful aspect in the home life of bright and bookish Opal is her father's passion to become a writer. Opal has total faith in his ability to succeed so, when he gets a seemingly positive response from a publisher, she, like him, is sure that he will soon achieve his dream. Father sends back the revisions that have been requested in the certain anticipation of becoming published. How significantly the family's status will be changed by this success is poignantly shown in how much nicer Opal's mother is to her father as well as how recklessly he begins to spend money, with tragic consequences for all. When Opal's world collapses as a result, her father reveals he was too ashamed to let the family know that he couldn't make it as a writer. Written in the frenzied climate of today, it feels as if Jacqueline Wilson is making a point about the pressure that wanting or needing to succeed can have.

This background demonstrates the very measurable changes in how children are finding books and the far larger role that the writers and illustrators themselves are playing in it as advocates for reading and as characters in their own books. Both of these are further influenced by the changing role of children in society in terms of their status within families. Though it would be an exaggeration to say they are equal partners in families, they are far more likely to be given the opportunity to make their own decisions in all respects than their parents or children from any previous generation.

As readers, this means they are making their own choices about what they read. Even for children who have only limited direct access to authors in ways described above, the route from book to reader has been radically changed by the opportunities of mass communication and also by the recognition that children find the books they want to read through their peers. Together, these have allowed the book to 'connect' with potential readers without the help of the many adult opinion formers or gatekeepers such as parents, teachers and librarians – all of whom could be useful sources of advice but could equally be somewhat traditional and backwards-looking in their choices.

As one of the most successful embodiments of the changing connection between writer and reader, Jacqueline Wilson draws on it in her writing. She represents writers with increasing frequency, most fully in *Clean Break* (2005), and in so doing gives an insightful commentary on the part current children's writers, including herself, are playing in developing children as readers and writers.

Jacqueline Wilson's success is now well established. A few measures are: her international sales figures have topped 45 million copies; she famously bounced Catherine Cookson off the coveted top spot as the most borrowed author from libraries – according to the Public Lending Right figures – and kept the crown in future years; she has been made a Dame of the British Empire (the first such for a children's author); she was Children's Laureate from 2005–7; and she has won almost every available award, including the Guardian Children's Fiction Prize for *The Illustrated Mum* (1999) in 2000. Her place in the academic study of children's literature and her contribution as a teacher of creative writing was confirmed in 2013 with her appointment as a Professorial Fellow at the University of Roehampton, London where she teaches modules in both the Children's Literature and the Creative Writing master's degree programmes. The University honoured her further by appointing her Chancellor from August 2014.

But, despite all of the above, there remain those who question Wilson's literary contribution to children's books. The children's librarians of the UK have never awarded her the prestigious and coveted CILIP Carnegie medal, for example. More surprising is that the respect and understanding from the parents of the children, girls in the most part, who love her so much has eluded her. The former appear to find her chatty first person narratives and simple use of vocabulary un-literary while the latter easily slip into thinking that because she shows children living in challenging situations she does not provide enough aspiration for the better off and more achieving children in the current success-oriented culture of childhood.

These omissions overlook Wilson's avowed commitment to encouraging children to read. She says it frequently in public but it is also very evident in her books where she refers constantly to children reading and has described one of her ambitions in her books as being to 'introduce children to writers who they wouldn't have thought of'. It is something she does in simple ways, like many other authors, by using her characters to link to her favourite books such as Noel Streatfeild's *Ballet Shoes* and E. Nesbit's *Five Children and It*. But she also goes well beyond this.

In *The Story of Tracy Beaker* (1991), a book which is fore-grounded for being about a child in a children's home, in addition to her key characteristics of distressed behaviour resulting in a reputation for being unmanageable, Tracy wants to be a writer. Given the known concerns about levels of literacy among children in care, this is already a statement. Wilson takes it further; a writer comes to visit the children's home. In keeping with her general outlook on life, Tracy Beaker is very suspicious of the writer. She thinks her name, Cam, is silly; she doesn't think she can be a writer because 'she didn't look a bit like a proper writer'; she thinks she is not even properly grown up as she bites her nails; she's sure she'll be like all the other adults who visit the home and patronise the children by telling them what they are thinking and feeling. But Cam gives the children time and gradually even suspicious Tracy is drawn into the group. It doesn't make her happy or change her behaviour in an instant – in fact the author's visit ends with Tracy starting a massive fight because one of the other children mocks her writing – but back in her room she writes and writes and writes. Cam has affected Tracy's behaviour; her being a writer has liberated Tracy and allows her to write. It is a constructive alternative to the destruction which is Tracy's usual response to conflict. She even develops a bump on her middle finger – one of Wilson's own trademarks of being a writer – which Nick Sharratt illustrates graphically.

The story, and Wilson's self-reference, draws on her considerable experience of communicating with children directly. Long before adults took notice of her books, she had forged her own bonds with children largely through making a spectacular number of school visits, 'holding a lot of sticky hands and being given cake', as she described it, where she meets 'outsider' children such as Tracy Beaker. She had observed at first-hand how a writer – an adult who had no known place in the hierarchies which some children had come to distrust – could have a particular and empowering impact.

Having spent years encouraging reading and writing within the everyday space of school and home, Wilson took a new tack in *Clean Break*. It reflected her own and others' altered status as writers and the role they now played as 'celebrities'. The changing status, though sometimes seen as inflated and a little unreal, was important in that it repositioned the creating of children's books and therefore the reading of them. The promotion and discussion of the most successful children's writers moved from library journals to broadsheet papers while meeting the authors moved from classrooms to tents for 1,000 at festivals such as the Hay Literary Festival. The author as the brand became the mantra for publishers. Children dragged their parents towards their favourite authors.

For no-one was this more true than for Wilson. While in classrooms across the country her style had long been quietly imitated by the young writers who were her enthusiastic readers, she became the brand as much as the books. Children wanted to meet her; she famously holds the record as the most queued-for author at a festival. She regularly speaks to over 5,000 children a year and she has an online following of 375,000. Wilson's persona is as popular as her books. In terms of her style and her engagement with children she has managed to remain almost unchanged in the quarter century of her success. Her direct communication with her readers whether in person or online has contributed significantly to her popularity and to her sales.

If Wilson only drew on her experiences and hinted at herself in *The Story of Tracy Beaker*, she takes a completely self-referring approach in *Clean Break*. Em, a typical Wilson character, is an unhappy child in a fractured family who finds refuge in reading and writing. Her favourite author is Jenna Williams whose books include 'Elsie No-Home', 'Forever Friends' and 'The Emerald Sisters'. As Wilson confesses in the introduction, 'The thought popped into my head that maybe she'd choose my books. Yet I couldn't actually put that in *Clean Break*. It would sound horribly like showing off. So I decided to invent an alternative me, Jenna Williams. We'd share the same initials and write very similar books.' Wilson then adds an extra joke for her reader, 'I wrote *The Diamond Girls* and old copycat Jenna wrote The Emerald Sisters.' Also in the introduction, she explains that the nice man who helps Em gets her books ready to be signed is in reality her driver Bob, an essential part of Wilson's demanding and complex role as a celebrity.

It is as a celebrity that Wilson now portrays her writer. On a day out in London all Em wants is to meet Jenna Williams. Carrying a sack of her books and those of her friend as well as her notebook with her own writing in it, she drags her family to the Jenna Williams signing session (interesting that by now the author isn't even associated with reading or writing but is seen as a person who signs, while the length of the queue rather than any other quality is the measure of success). Gran groans when seeing the queue. "For pity's sake, we can't hang around here all day, Em! We'll be hours and hours!" said Gran. Later she adds, "She's just some boring middle-aged lady with a funny haircut. What's so special about her?" But Em remains determined and they queue for over three hours. When Em finally gets to meet Jenna Williams she is 'agonisingly shy' until the author asks, "Can I see your story for a minute, Emily?" Emily hands over the story and Jenna Williams turns the tables: "It looks wonderful, Emily! It's such a great idea. Watch out! I might put it in one of my books!" The role of reader and writer is momentarily transposed as Em considers the possibilities this raises before Jenna Williams, picking up on Em's love of pretending, confirms, "I think you're definitely going to be a writer yourself one day, Emily."

In this acknowledged text self-portrait – also heavily confirmed by Nick Sharratt's illustrations – Wilson's meta-fiction shows that although the trappings of the writer have changed, her role as educator and inspirer of reading and writing has not. In fact, the elevated status of the writer raises the status of reading and writing. Now dressed in the garments of fame and money and positioned appropriately rather than in the world of education, Wilson shows children as readers and writers and the writers that inspire them as highly successful. It is an upwards spiral of success; both sides are achievers with all the signifiers that entails in a modern world.

In the examples of both *The Story of Tracy Beaker* and *Clean Break*, one more glossily than the other, Wilson's accurate depiction of the reality of the role writers play in the literacy experience of their readers shows the purpose and power of reading and writing as being nothing less than a transformational change from rags to riches, both emotionally and financially. Written almost fifteen years apart and charting her own journey and highlighting of impact of writers on readers, in *The Story of Tracy Beaker* Wilson hints that a child in a children's home may find greater emotional equilibrium after meeting a writer whereas in *Clean Break* she makes a bolder statement that a writer can affirm the ambition of a child who wants to write with the subliminal message that she too may then swap domestic strife for the comfort of life full of success – and a driver!

Primary sources

Hill, Eric. *Where's Spot?* [1980]. London: Picture Puffin, 2009.
McKee, David. *Elmer* [1989]. London: Anderson Press, 2007.
Nesbit, E. *Five Children and It* [1902]. Ware: Wordsworth Editions, 1993.
Nesbit, E. *The Railway Children* [1906]. Harmonsworth: Penguin, 1970.
Rowling, J. K. *Harry Potter and the Philosopher's Stone*. London: Bloomsbury, 1997.
Sedgwick, Markus. *She is not Invisible*. London: Orion, 2013.
Streatfeild, Noel. *Ballet Shoes*. London: J. M. Dent and Sons, 1936.
Wilson, Jacqueline. *Clean Break*. London: Doubleday, 2005.
Wilson, Jacqueline. *Opal Plumstead*. London: Doubleday, 2014.
Wilson, Jacqueline. *The Illustrated Mum*. London: Doubleday, 1999.
Wilson, Jacqueline. *The Story of Tracy Beaker*. London: Doubleday, 1991.

Secondary sources

BookTrust. *A Celebration of Writing Together 2001–2007*, 2007. Print.

BookTrust. Everybody Writes 2009–2011. http://www.booktrust.org.uk/programmes/primary/everybody-writes/. Online.

DfEE. *The National Literacy Strategy: A Framework for Teaching*. London: HMSO, 1998.

Hahn, Daniel, Flynn, Leonie and Reuben, Susan. *The Ultimate Book Guide*. London: A. C. Black, 2004. Print.

Horner, Sue. *Magic Dust That Lasts*. Arts Council, 2010. Available at http://www.artscouncil.org.uk/media/uploads/Writers_in_schools.pdf Online.

Wilson, Jacqueline. *Great Books to Read Aloud*. London: Corgi Children's Books, 2006. Print.

9

'WHAT ELSE CAN THIS BOOK DO?'

Picturebooks as stage sets for acts of reading

Mary Anne Wolpert and Morag Styles

Prologue

L: Who is that?

CLAIRE: Herb.

DAVID: No! It's Goldilocks!

[*All laughing*]

DAVID: [*Pretending to be Herb trapped in the body of Goldilocks*] Oh my goodness, look at my hair!

[*All laughing*]

L: What is she doing here?

CLAIRE: She's writing, she's writing.

DAVID: I can't stand my hair, please send a hairdresser!

[*All laughing*]

CLAIRE: She's writing because she wants to be the best star. [*Reads from the cover*] 'The divinely …'

ELLIE: I love Lauren Child [*She takes the book and kisses it*]

DAVID: She could jump out of it and kiss you on the lips!

[*All laughing*]

DAVID: If pictures are real and people can jump out of books …

ELLIE: Yeah, that would be so cool! And they will come alive … And then imagine it happen … Imagine!!

(from Louiza Mallouri's research in Arizpe and Styles 2008,
pp. 212–213)

This short exchange takes place between three children aged 7 and 8 discussing Lauren Child's *Who's Afraid of the Big Bad Book?* is set up as a stage show from the covers in. There is an example of *mise en abyme* on the front cover, a dramatic

FIGURE 9.1

From *Who's Afraid of the Big Bad Book?* by Lauren Child. Published by Hodder Children's Books. Reprinted by permission of Hodder Children's Books.

double fold-out spread, several pages have to be viewed upside down, there are holes in the text, competing versions of character's viewpoints are expressed through different fonts, the typology itself is spectacular and intertextual references to fairy tales predominate … and so on – all of these typical features of postmodern picturebooks.

The *Big Bad Book* represents reading as playful, dynamic and interactive. The central character, Herb, gets into all sorts of scrapes because of his voracious and performative reading. Instead of imbibing the author's story, he physically engages with it – drawing on it, adding bits, even cutting up characters. Reading is anything but passive in *Big Bad Book* and this in turn, the evidence as cited above would suggest, encourages active responses in readers. If the book itself is a sort of stage set, readers are the actors that bring it to life.

McQuillan and Conde (1996) use the term 'ludic readers' (derived from the Latin *ludo*, I play), which serves to remind us that reading is 'at root a play activity, and usually paratelic, that is, pursued for its own sake' (Apter 1979, cited in Nell 1988, p. 7). The children above spontaneously used *Big Bad Book* as a sort of theatre on which to play out their own 'acts of reading'. Quentin Blake (2002) has talked about how he views a double page spread as a stage, and many other critics apply theatrical metaphors to picturebooks. In this chapter, we explore further examples of how reading is 'staged' in selected picturebooks from the past thirty years, showing how they have shaped new understandings of what we mean by reading, what this means for readers, and how reading can be enacted beyond the page.

How Texts Teach What Readers Learn by Margaret Meek (1988) was an early critical appreciation of the dynamic relationship between multilayered texts and their readers. Through careful analysis of a number of the key picturebooks of the time, she uncovered a complexity of literary and linguistic reference and showed how children used this to make meaning, and so, by means of the texts themselves, were taught to read dynamically. An important strand of Meek's argument was that how much sense children made of reading depended to a large extent on what they had read before and the significant role of intertextuality in picturebooks was highlighted throughout. As Hunt points out in chapter 2, intertextuality is an enduring feature of fiction for children and the books we discuss in this chapter are all imbued with references to other books and different forms of texts.

Beginning with *The Jolly Postman*, we consider the invitations, challenges and affordances offered by some significant picturebooks that span the last thirty years. In so doing, we draw attention to representations of acts of reading and reader response through our chosen examples. Deciding which picturebooks to select was extremely difficult: we have deliberately avoided some of those already much discussed (for example, picturebooks by Anthony Browne, John Burningham, Satoshi Kitamura, David Macaulay, David McKee, Maurice Sendak...) and we have also limited ourselves to well-known picturebooks by British or American illustrators. We try to demonstrate some of the challenges involved in reading sophisticated picturebooks like these and show how they require active participation and engagement and encourage agency in their young audience.

The First Act

The Jolly Postman steals the show

The authors of this chapter are old enough to remember the reception to Janet and Allan Ahlberg's *The Jolly Postman* in 1986. Children, teachers, scholars and critics alike were mesmerised by its originality; many educators within its adult audience were aware that this wonderfully playful text had changed forever the scope of what picturebooks could aspire to.

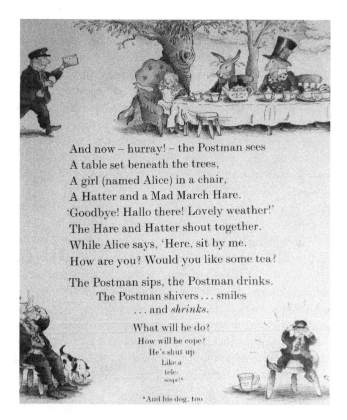

And now – hurray! – the Postman sees
A table set beneath the trees,
A girl (named Alice) in a chair,
A Hatter and a Mad March Hare.
'Goodbye! Hallo there! Lovely weather!'
The Hare and Hatter shout together.
While Alice says, 'Here, sit by me.
How are you? Would you like some tea?

The Postman sips, the Postman drinks.
The Postman shivers ... smiles
... and *shrinks*.

What will he do?
How will he cope?
He's shut up
Like a
tele-
scope!*

*And his dog, too

FIGURE 9.2

From *The Jolly Postman* by Allan and Janet Ahlberg. Published by Heinemann. Reprinted by permission of Heinemann.

Although pop-up books and sophisticated paper engineering were already familiar through inventive artists such as Jan Pienkowski, no-one had come up with such imaginative 'props' within a picturebook before, not only demanding physical interaction but expecting readers to draw on literary knowledge of traditional nursery rhymes and fairy tales. Indeed, the scope of intertextual reference was remarkable with probably the widest range of text-types up to that point, or perhaps since – letters, postcards, catalogues, tiny books, addressed envelopes, birthday cards, fairy tale retellings, invitations, newspapers, press statements, postage marks, recipes, circulars, brochures, advertisements, publicity logos, nursery rhymes, sayings ... And while children were delighting in playing with these texts, they were simultaneously embracing the wider culture of the society they lived in. Aesthetically the book was warm, colourful, reader-friendly with positive images of children, adults and storybook characters. Reading was represented as a joyful cornucopia linked to amusing social and literary events. Allan Ahlberg's inventive narrative focused on retelling fairy tales with a new, often humorous twist, and the different threads were pulled together through a rollicking narrative rhyme.

The Jolly Christmas Postman, a well-deserved Kate Greenaway winner, followed in 1991 with more of the same, exemplified this time by Christmas festivities as a backdrop with the addition of Father Christmas, Christmas cards and presents, jigsaws, etc. and a spectacular peep-show. When it might have seemed that nothing more could be done with the format, the Ahlbergs produced *The Jolly Pocket Postman* (1995), which featured even more creative and playful materials such as board games, songs and a magnifying glass. In terms of reading invitations, the scope was broadened to include a wide range of 'classic' fiction from Hans Andersen's fairy tales to both *Alice* books, *The Wizard of Oz*, *Peter Pan*, *The Wind in the Willows*, *A Child's Garden of Verses* and *Treasure Island*, *The Pied Piper of Hamlyn*, Tolkien's *Father Christmas Letters* and *Peter Rabbit*.

In the ten years between the publication of the first and third *Postman* picturebooks, the Ahlbergs had become more and more ingenious in terms of content but the basic premise didn't change. Interestingly, the books appeared at a time when the climate in British schools still included imaginative approaches to learning to read and a strong interest in 'real books'. The stranglehold of synthetic phonics as the main approach to reading in the early years – and all that signified in terms of schools' purchase of picturebooks – then high, now much reduced – had not yet begun.

Act Two

The True Story tells some lies

Three years after the first *Jolly Postman* book came the equally ground-breaking *The True Story of the Three Little Pigs! By A. Wolf* by Jon Scieszka and Lane Smith (1989). Some of the same tropes were there as in the *Jolly Postman*; no movable parts this time, but an even more sophisticated book asking even more of its slightly older readership. One of the most striking features was its unusual and outstanding design, bringing 'all the visual and textual elements ... into a coherent, aesthetically pleasing whole', as Salisbury (2004) put it. This is also true of the later collaborations between Smith and Scieszka which followed this debut and for which Molly Leach, their exceptional designer, should be commended.

The True Story demonstrated a witty and ironic relationship between word and image, its main thrust questioning certainties about the authority of text. The reading matter is untrustworthy from the front cover onwards where the written text, apparently provided by Alexander T. Wolf in newsprint format, but sounding mightily like Raymond Chandler's much loved literary detective, Philip Marlowe, is being read by a well-dressed pig. Therein lies the fun, but the serious point behind it alludes to issues of power and unreliable narratives as what the narrator has to say is undermined by counterpointing imagery (Nikolajeva and Scott 2006 [2001]). This time a well-known tale is not only played with, as in the work of the Ahlbergs, but totally subverted – being told from two opposing viewpoints that can only be understood by reading the interplay between words and pictures.

FIGURE 9.3

From *The True Story of the Three Little Pigs!* by Jon Scieszka and Lane Smith. Published by Viking. Reprinted by permission of Viking Books.

Furthermore, the sheer complexity of intertextual references to other stories, which include popular early twentieth century detective fiction for adults, alongside the traditional tale of the wolf and three pigs, is made much more intense as it is accompanied by equally rich and demanding illustrations. For example, while the newspaper format of the story indicated by the cover suggests that this is a factual and authoritative narrative, subsequent pictures are somewhat blurred, rather like flash-backs providing a hazy recollection of events. This slightly surreal element is enhanced by distorted images mixed up with cuttings from real photographs etc. As for the frames, some characters break out of them, suggesting a lack of boundaries between what is thought to be real and what is fantasy.

If the illustrations in *The True Story* were aesthetically rich, innovative and not obviously friendly to a young audience, this was even more apparent with each new book from this highly creative team. *The Stinky Cheese Man* (1992) breaks just about every rule and could be described as the ultimate metafictive text, since every page questions how the text is constructed. It is a totally unreliable, unstable text with picturebook conventions turned (sometimes literally) upside down and most assumptions about what books are and how to read them are contested. The authors show huge respect for young readers in that they are expected to work very hard to make sense of what is happening. The design and the content are inseparable with a

dialogue going on between characters and the page itself, while bizarre and complicated illustrations often make reference to art movements of the twentieth century,
such as cubism. It is impossible to make sense of this book without a performative
response and young readers engaged in the story can be seen turning the book
upside down, moving pages backwards and forwards to check out characters' utter-
ances, let alone the need to compare their knowledge of traditional tales with the
subversive goings on in *The Stinky Cheese Man*. Any normal story expectations of
climax or resolution are destabilised by the actors who do anything but the
expected – and therein lies the fun.

Squids will be Squids (1998) is equally original. This time the endpapers make
intratextual references to previous picturebooks by Smith and Scieszka, as well as
referring to Bewick's famous illustrations of nature in the eighteenth century. As the
book is an ingenious contemporary 'take' on Aesop's fables, the authors provide
historical interest in their use of early script typeface and information about Aesop
himself, if somewhat exaggerated and played for laughs. Instead of old tales changed,
we actually have new and absurd yet hilarious fables accompanied by clever, ground-
breaking art work and design.

The distance Scieszka and Smith have travelled in ten years is quite phenomenal
and we have only drawn attention here to a small portion of their output. That same
distance has also had to be scaled by their readers who are expected to be capable of
manipulating sophisticated literacy skills and draw on knowledge of literature and
art history in order to begin to fathom the affordances of these picturebooks. In
other words, the intertextual references apply not only to text and what readers
have read before, but also to what they have *seen* before. Smith and Scieszka's picturebooks demand creative acts of reading; they clearly believe in the intelligence
of young readers and the popularity of their books suggest that such trust is not
misplaced.

Act Three

Big bad Wolves

Emily Gravett's debut picturebook won the Kate Greenaway Award in 2005. In
Wolves – a book which, we are informed on the inside front fold, follows the
'National Carroticulum' – a naive rabbit visits a library and 'burrows' a book about
wolves. The book is packed with further textual puns and visual jokes and a remov-
able letter and library ticket add to the physical and interactive act of reading.
Characters and events seemingly escape from the pages of the text while the
absorbed Rabbit is so busy with his nose buried in the book that he fails to see
the dangers around him, although readers may be aware of these immediately. By
the time Rabbit has discovered that wolves might not be the creatures of fairy tales
whose favourite food is 'small girls in red hoods', it is too late; an overdue notice
from the library lies on his doormat with other unread mail at Lane's End Burrow
in Nibbleswick. To be in on the act and 'get' the joke at the end, the reader needs an

understanding of how to use a library, to realise that the library book the rabbit is reading is the same *Wolves* that the reader has in their hands and that the library card and the official letter on the final endpapers indicate a less than happy outcome for Rabbit. In fact, at least four different versions of the physical text are suggested and the whole book is 'untrustworthy', blurring the boundaries between fiction and reality, in 'appealing and entertaining ways' (Mackey 2008, p. 109). In the light of many recent closures of public libraries in England, it is interesting that, in this inventive twenty-first century picture book, the author stages her narrative centrally within the setting of an old fashioned library which is without the contemporary additions of online, digitalised services.

Gravett's *Little Mouse's Big Book of Fears* (2007), another Kate Greenaway Award winner, is a stunningly clever and appealing book using many of the features ascribed to previous illustrators we have mentioned in new and inventive ways. Firstly, it is a wonderfully comforting book for the child who is unlikely to know the technical, Latin words given to the various real, and amusingly invented phobias but who can identify with the terrified mouse and share his concerns. In addition, like the Ahlbergs, Gravett combines a range of non-fiction text types – albums, scrapbooks, dictionaries, greetings cards, posters, newspapers, advertisements and maps – asking of young readers an understanding of a variety of textual conventions and forms. The book demands interaction. It is a hugely physical text, with holes to put fingers through, pages that are half-eaten, torn, smudged and messy, flaps to lift and items to pull out. The reader's mandate, as Goldstone (2008, p. 120) notes, is clear:

> think about this story so it makes sense. Do not be shy, be a co-author. Feel free to play with the story, add to it and alter it!

Readers are encouraged from the endpapers in to take centre stage and add to the construction of the text as it unfolds:

> Each page in this book provides a large blank space
> For you to record and face your fear using a combination of:
>
> Drawing
> Writing
> Collage.

On every spread thereafter readers are invited to 'use the space below to record your fears' whilst the mouse's anxieties are recorded in a child-like script. The pencil of the little mouse/child actually wears down to a chewed off stub as the fears are catalogued. The certificate of bravery on the final page is left blank for the reader to record their name and what they have been 'very VERY brave about,' suggesting that this act of reading, and of writing, is a live, interactive performance with the finale left for the reader to decide.

Act Four

Huffing and puffing the story apart

Though any of the most original picturebooks by this notable author could have served our purpose, David Wiesner's Caldecott Medal winner, *The Three Pigs* (2001) offers particularly dramatic perspectives on play, performativity and physicality involved in reading complex multimodal texts. This brilliant metafictive narrative challenges basic assumptions about what a text is and explores inventively the relationship between author, narrator and reader. Expectations are set up, both verbally and visually on the title page and first two double spreads that this is going to be the conventional story of the three little pigs. These are literally, blown apart by the third spread when the first pig is huffed and puffed 'right out of the story.' To make sense of the narrative, it is necessary for readers to grapple with the notion of story as a construct – that it is created and can be changed. The pigs are blown out of the physical confines of the frames of the book and then reconstructed on the picture panels, using them to fly into other stories from other eras and rescue various story-book characters created in different artistic styles. Through speech bubbles, readers overhear the pigs' conversations with each other as they comment on their adventures and discuss how to navigate their various scenarios so that the script is forever changing in ways

FIGURE 9.4

that cannot be anticipated. White space is used to indicate the transition between these events as the pigs fly on the paper planes they have constructed from the pages of the original text and images into different stories which have distinctive aesthetic styles to represent their different modes. Finally even the words of the narrative, which have continued to mimic the style of a traditional story, dissolve and are reassembled by the pigs with that big bad wolf inserting himself into the script.

Sipe and Brightman (2006) found in their research that very young readers are able to interpret the space between stories and their narrators, enjoying the subversion of expectation and boundaries. In their interpretation of *The Three Pigs*, these six year old children were aware of the theatrical entrances and exits of the pigs, and also responded to the characters' performance on the page with their own active interjections. Pantaleo (2004) too demonstrates how Grade 1 readers were aware of the 'digressions, gaps and disruptions' (p. 182) in the book and that the pigs themselves had to construct their own endings. She concludes that texts such as these 'demand a higher level of sophistication and complexity with respect to gap-filling (Iser 1978) and predicting' (pp. 186–187). Twenty years on from the Ahlbergs, the journey that Wiesner makes both characters and readers travel takes them through increasingly unstable narrative territory and provides new perspectives about the construction of narratives and the role of readers in interacting with them. As Nodelman (1988) notes, readers are expected to become meaning-makers able to make sense out of an increasingly complex catalogue of 'codes, conventions, assumptions and interpretative strategies' (p. 35). *The Three Pigs* is arguably the most demanding picturebook of all those we have chosen in this chapter.

Act Five

Playing with Traction Man

Meek (1991) offered us significant insights into the relationship between play, narrative and reading, arguing that reading itself is a form of deep play and that through such play, children learn about the power of narrative and of text. Mini Grey's *Traction Man is Here* (2005) is a text that embodies how play and performance can be represented as an integral part of the act of reading in a picturebook. Throughout *Traction Man*, an unnamed child is absorbed in small world play and, through humour, irony and parody, Grey invokes an irresistible representation of the private world of children's imagination and sense of theatre. As Nikolajeva comments in the first chapter of this volume, whilst there are texts that do not overtly show children actually reading, the characters represented within them have familiarity with stories and act them out in their games. This is clearly evident in *Traction Man*. Through playing with his Traction Man toy in a variety of everyday situations, the child within the text becomes the narrator. Mundane events such as washing up and having a bath are manipulated and enlivened with dramatic effect, inviting young readers to also actively engage with, and bring their own creativity to story-telling and the experience of reading.

FIGURE 9.5
From *Traction Man Is Here* by Mini Grey. Published by Red Fox. Reprinted by permission of
The Random House Group Ltd.

From the start, the cover invites readers to conceive of the text as a three-
dimensional box to open and play with. The title page establishes the context for the
story: an unsigned letter to Santa asks for a new Traction Man toy. Scattered writing
implements and child-like handwriting suggest a work in progress with the child
given agency as the creator of the text. Four scenes unfold in the first half of the
book in which Traction Man wears each of the four outfits depicted in the letter to
Santa. There are no further clues to suggest what further missions are in store.
Instead, events take an unpredictable turn when Traction Man's image as an action
hero is seemingly destroyed: the next outfit is an 'all-in-one knitted green romper
suit and matching bonnet.' Inventiveness and imagination come to the rescue as
Traction Man and Scrubbing Brush turn this fashion disaster to their advantage, save
some crashed young spoons and, in true superhero movie style, on the final spread

are left to savour their triumphs, basking on a book (*Biggles gets his Men*) on a sea-blue carpet, 'ready for Anything'. The visual presence of the evil, grinning scissors on the verso suggests that there is indeed another adventure in store. Humour permeates the book, through word, image and the interplay between them. There are many intertextual references, particularly to superhero stories both of written and film narratives that can enrich readers' engagement with the book if, as Sipe (2002) argues, they can make hermeneutic and aesthetic connections, entering the books to play, perform and create.

Finale

The book takes a final bow

The picturebooks we have exemplified so far have raised many questions about what a text is and how reading can be perceived. However, we cannot conclude this chapter without acknowledging how authors/illustrators of recent picturebooks have explored the affordances the format offers to present new interpretations of how reading can be staged in the light of the brave new world of apps and digital texts. Therefore we begin our finale with an example of such a text before returning to two examples of recent books that champion 'what else' books can do for young readers.

In Hervé Tullet's playful boardbook *Press Here* (2011) the narrator/author is seemingly involved in direct conversation with the reader and a physically interactive experience is created. Readers are invited to tap, stroke, rub, tilt, shake and blow on the coloured dots to 'change the illustrations on each page'. The dots don't move, of course. However, the text suggests that there is a dialogue with the reader and that readers' actions are changing the illustration. The bright primary colours and textures used to create the coloured dots are suggestive of finger painting and evoke a sense of early childhood play. The visual and physical similarity with iPads and phone apps, along with the accompanying trailer, website and app in this board book format extends the range of texts young children encounter.

In sharp aesthetic contrast, Oliver Jeffers's *The Incredible Book Eating Boy* (2006) presents a dull colour palette, dominated by brown and grey tones. As well as visual and verbal jokes on book titles and publishers' conventions and genres from exercise books to dictionary entries, *Book Eating Boy* features a variety of mainly old print types that are literally gobbled up by the protagonist. Initially he is regarded as a phenomenon, appearing on stage in a vaudeville-like act once he can 'eat a whole book in one go.' The humour lies in it being a funny idea in the first place and in the book-eating leading to plenty of metaphorical burping and farting. The bite-shaped piece missing at the end indicates a final physical interaction between the protagonist and the book, whilst the exhortation on the back cover: 'Please DO NOT try to EAT this BOOK at home' invites the reader to reflect further on the underlying message in Jeffers's text. This is serious: books make you smarter and help you get on in the world and readers also need to take time to get most out of them.

Lane Smith's *It's a Book!* (2011) is a powerful battle-cry for the book that champions the value of a physical book against the appeal of technology. If we return to the Ahlbergs for a moment, reading their books requires engagement with a huge variety of text types, whereas *It's a Book!* is pared down to its essentials in every way, including the fact that it only makes reference to a single text from the literary canon – *Treasure Island*. It is also pared down visually in comparison to the Ahlbergs with austere design, an earth-coloured palette and a deliberately old-fashioned style. However, the performative element is given a high profile in the amusing interaction between the two characters. The clash of cultures between what a book made of paper can do in comparison to slick, high tech, digital reading material cleverly shows the limitations of the latter by pin-pointing the simple but lasting qualities of a book.

In the title for our chapter we ask: 'What else can this book do?' The quotation is taken, of course, from *It's a Book!* which demonstrates that, without any gimmicks, a book can do just about everything that matters to keen readers: offer wonderful stories, provide deep engagement and be durable, lasting and easily transportable. You don't require any extras, 'Jackass!' – just the reader, a good story and the imagination.

In this chapter we have tried to show how sophisticated picturebooks over the past thirty years have consistently challenged our understanding of texts and reading in contemporary life. We have acknowledged the competition books for children face in the light of new technologies. We have also emphasised the huge creativity shown by illustrators resulting in the rich variety of inventive picturebooks available for children. In return, the enthusiastic and intelligent response of their young audience brings hope that whatever happens in the world of picturebook publishing and education, young readers will continue to find their way to pleasurable, playful and performative acts of reading in whatever form or context visual texts present themselves.

Primary sources

Ahlberg, Allan and Janet. *The Jolly Postman or Other People's Letters*. London: Heinemann, 1986.

Ahlberg, Allan and Janet. *The Jolly Christmas Postman*. London: Heinemann, 1991.

Ahlberg, Allan and Janet. *The Jolly Pocket Postman*. London: Heinemann, 1995.

Child, Lauren. *Who's Afraid of the Big Bad Book?* London: Hodder Children's Books, 2002.

Gravett, Emily. *Wolves*. London: Macmillan, 2005.

Gravett, Emily. *Little Mouse's Big Book of Fears*. London: Macmillan, 2007.

Grey, Mini. *Traction Man Is Here*. London: Jonathan Cape, 2005.

Jeffers, Oliver. *The Incredible Book Eating Boy*. London: HarperCollins, 2006.

Scieszka, Jon and Smith, Lane. *The True Story of the Three Little Pigs!* New York: Viking Press, 1989.

Scieszka, Jon and Smith, Lane. *The Stinky Cheese Man and Other Fairly Stupid Tales*. New York: Viking Press, 1992.

Scieszka, Jon and Smith, Lane. *Squids will be Squids*. New York: Viking Press, 1998.

Smith, Lane. *It's a Book!* London: Macmillan Children's Books, 2011.
Tullet, Hervé. *Press Here.* San Francisco: Chronicle Books, 2011.
Wiesner, David. *The Three Pigs.* New York: Clarion Books, 2001.

Secondary sources

Arizpe, Evelyn and Styles, Morag with Cowan, Kate, Mallouri, Louiza, and Wolpert, Mary Anne. 'The Voices Behind the Pictures: Children Responding to Postmodern Picturebooks'. In L. R. Sipe and S. Pantaleo (Eds.), *Postmodern Picturebooks. Play, Parody and Self-Referentiality* (pp. 207–222). London: Routledge, 2008.

Blake, Quentin. *Laureate's Progress.* London: Random House, 2002.

Goldstone, Bette. 'The Paradox of Space in Postmodern Picturebooks'. In L. R. Sipe and S. Pantaleo (Eds.), *Postmodern Picturebooks. Play, Parody and Self-Referentiality* (pp. 117–129). London: Routledge, 2008.

Iser, Wolfgang. *The Act of Reading: A Theory of Aesthetic Response.* Baltimore and London: The Johns Hopkins University Press, 1978.

Mackey, Margaret. 'Postmodern Picture Books and the Material Conditions of Reading'. In L. R. Sipe and S. Pantaleo (Eds.), *Postmodern Picturebooks. Play, Parody and Self-Referentiality* (pp. 103–116). London: Routledge, 2008.

Meek, Margaret. *How Texts Teach what Readers Learn.* Stroud: Thimble Press, 1988.

Meek, Margaret. *On Being Literate.* London: The Bodley Head, 1991.

McQuillan, Jeff and Conde, Gisela. 'The Conditions of Flow in Reading: Two Studies of Optimal Experience'. *Reading Psychology: An International Quarterly, 17,* 109–135. 1996.

Nell, Victor. 'The Psychology of Reading for Pleasure: Needs and Gratifications', *Reading Research Quarterly, 23*(1), 6–46. 1988.

Nikolajeva, Maria and Scott, Carole. *How Picturebooks Work.* London: Routledge, 2001 [new edition 2006].

Nodelman, Perry. *Words about Pictures: The Narrative Art of Children's Picture books.* Athens, GA: University of Georgia Press, 1988.

Pantaleo, Sylvia. 'Young Children and Radical Change Characteristics in Picture Books'. *The Reading Teacher, 58*(2), 178–187. 2004.

Salisbury, Martin. *Illustrating Children's Books: Creating Pictures for Publication.* London: A. and C. Black, 2004.

Sipe, Lawrence R. 'Talking Back and Talking Over: Young Children's Expressive Engagement During Storybooks Read-alouds'. *The Reading Teacher, 55*(5), 476–483. 2002.

Sipe, Lawrence R. and Brightman, Anne E. 'Teacher Scaffolding of First-graders' Literary Understanding During Readalouds of Fairytale Variants'. *Yearbook of the National Reading Conference, 55,* 279–292. 2006.

10

UNCOVERING READER EXPECTATIONS AND CONCEPTS OF READERS IN CHILDREN'S LITERATURE OF THE DIGITAL AGE

Sylvia Warnecke

Much of what research celebrates as the advantages and exciting aspects of new media is nothing new to children's literature. Features such as the ubiquity of images, an emphasis on the interrelation of image and text, hybridity, genre blurring, narrative disruptions, self-referentiality and parody, interactivity, intertextuality and multimodality have been aspects of fiction written for children and young adults for decades (Evangelia 2011). At a time, when computers and other digital media have become a common facet of our own and our children's lives, there appears to be – at first glance – a curious absence of technology in children's books. It is only a few genres such as cartoons, graphic novels, ghost stories or dystopian Young Adult fiction that present these technologies as an established motif and focal point of plot.

Yet the growing interpenetration of narratives for children in different modes and the fast development of reading in diverse formats cannot be denied. For example, Scholastic's biennial survey of 6- to 17-year-olds' reading in 2013 found the popularity of e-books soaring as the number of surveyed children who said they had read an e-book had increased from 25 to 46 per cent in only three years (Gewertz 2013, p. 8). This finding goes hand in hand with Mackey's observation that '[w]e now live in a new era of multiple systems of recorded symbolic representation, readily accessible to many of even the youngest readers' (2003, p. 592), as appliances such as e-readers and tablet computers are extensively used for a wide range of purposes by people of all ages in the Western world and beyond.

At the same time, the creation of texts in traditional as well as digital publishing for children is becoming progressively diverse. On the one hand, there are the remediation of printbooks as audiobooks, e-books, enhanced e-books, or video books and the rapidly increasing range of story-based apps for children. On the other hand, there are born digital narratives, stand-alone or as a part of immersive virtual environments, along with more and more complex digital games based on narrative approaches that enable players to determine plot development. Then there is the influence of these new modes of storytelling on structural and aesthetic idiosyncrasies of children's fiction, also on those works in print format.

Mackey confirms that these developments also have an effect on how young people read and engage with narratives today when she states that 'reading now exists as part of what we might perhaps best consider a multifaceted performance space and thinking space, [... yet the] virtues of print have not been overturned or replaced but they are in the process of being augmented' (2011, p. 99). Her statement addresses widespread concerns about possible negative impacts of the advance of digital technologies on children's reading and highlights the need for a revised understanding of reading and readers in the digital age.

In the context of the developments outlined above, this chapter investigates expectations revolving around texts that are influenced by the advance of digital technologies. A particular focus will be on how readers' expectations of these hybrid stories, as well as expectations of the reader as represented in the text, are portrayed. Three case studies form the basis of this chapter. Case study one examines Reif Larsen's *The Selected Works of T. S. Spivet* (2009) to highlight how narratives in print format can be augmented by replicating online practices of meaning-making. The second case study revolving around Scholastic's *The 39 Clues* series establishes the place of reading and the role of the reader in immersive virtual environments. The third case study focusing on the born digital narrative *Inanimate Alice* by BradField Productions (2005–2014) investigates how the blurring of the boundaries between different artistic genres and roles and between the narrative and the virtual world impacts on the portrayal of expectations of reading and imbues readers with agency.

Blurring the boundaries between print and digital narrative, between reality and fiction: Reif Larsen's *The Selected Works of T. S. Spivet*

Larsen's novel documents the coming of age of T. S. Spivet, a child, having grown up in a remote place with little experience of the world, who goes on a journey of discovery, secretly and on his own. He is a '12-year-old prodigy with a compulsion to make maps of movement, geographical and sociological phenomena, emotions and historical developments' (Adams 2009, np). Although each step of his voyage is meticulously mapped by the protagonist, his journey's movement is not easy to track as the reader actually joins T. S. on two journeys – the voyage to Washington in order to receive an award for his mapping skills at the Smithsonian Institute; and his inner passage to adulthood, identifying his role in the Spivet family and the world at large. What becomes apparent during both journeys is that understanding the world means dealing with aspects far beyond the confines of ostensibly scientific maps. Hence T. S.'s mapping, exposed as a mental and emotional need, is characterised by the paradox that his search for accuracy and scientific validation leads to the discovery of disorder and ambiguity.

The paratexts of the novel leave the reader in no doubt that the maps presented throughout the story question the concept of 'real' places and things. The first page, a mock-medieval 'map' of the globe, is adorned with a motto from Herman Melville's *Moby Dick*: 'It is not down in any map; true places never are' (np). This is the first of many instances that challenge readers' expectations, as they are invited to consider the tension between reality and fiction at the very point of embarking on reading this novel. The paratext at the end revisits *Moby Dick* in that it shows characters from Melville's novel in a world that appears to be dissolving around them. In the midst of the disarray of lines and curves the reader finds just this one statement: 'Everything is fiction' (np). This paratext provides the solution to the riddle of the paratext at the start as it highlights that even the 'true places' we inhabit and those well-known places T. S. visits in the course of his journey can also be regarded as fictional, fantastic and extraordinary; commanding the reader to take a stance and decide on her very own understanding of the tension between reality and fiction.

The very start of T. S.'s first-person narrative drives home the message to the reader that, even when growing up, the distinction between reality and fiction is difficult or in fact impossible. He points out that growing up taught him a crucial lesson about this which helped him understand the world and the inherent contradiction in his mapping of it. T.S. states that the crudeness of the map of 'shaking God's hand' on Mount Humbug 'was not only due to the shaky hands of youth but also because I did not understand that the map of a place was different from the place itself. At age six, a boy could enter the world of a map just as easily as the genuine article' (p. 8). This statement along with the paratext highlights the expectation of the reader, in fact the reader's task, to actively question any recorded symbolic representation of the world and to develop her own understanding of it by making connections between the fictional narrative and her personal experiences. That is to say, the reader is challenged to understand that each recorded representation of the world is the expression of an individual's understanding of it, which can be markedly different from any other individual's experience. This is particularly pertinent at a time when recorded visual representations of the world surrounding the reader have become just as pervasive as those using words, when everyone can produce and publish visual images of 'real things' with ease.

The reading experience of this novel is highly contemporary and defies readers' expectations of how to read a fictional narrative. It demands navigation through plots and side plots presented in words and images as well as understanding their (un-)connectedness. The contemporary character of the narrative is created by text and images that are intertwined in multiple ways. On the page, the main narrative is surrounded by pictorial and verbal commentary in the form of annotated maps in the margins. T. S.'s maps, visually representing his impressions and interpretation of the events he narrates, are linked with single sentences or entire paragraphs on the page by dotted lines and arrows. Again and again, the maps encroach on the text, even take centre stage and push the written words of the narrative to the margins.

This phenomenon has a twofold effect on the reading process. Initially, it slows down the reader, forcing her to carefully consider all aspects of the narrative. Secondly, reader expectations are countered, as the reader has to make decisions about how to read this novel and determine which of these maps and the associated commentary in the margins to take into account. The first part of the novel can be read and followed without taking the maps into account. As the story progresses, the connections between the maps and the narrative, and between the maps themselves grow more and more complex, reflecting the increasing life experience and mapping skills of the first-person narrator.

As a next step, the reader must grasp the meaning of the maps, defying expectations of maps as visual representations of 'real things and places'. The maps offer information about the emotional and mental state of the protagonist, which has to be decoded by the reader depending on her own life experiences. The reader also has to resolve how and at what point of reading the individual page she engages with the maps; i.e. immediately following the arrow to the map from the text, or looking at the maps first to make predictions about the narrative, or to read the narrative in a chronological order first to then follow it up by engaging with the maps.

Text and maps together broaden the reader's perspective by offering links to additional information and ideas on aspects of the narrative. The lines and arrows to the maps in the margin mirror hyperlinking in the world wide web, where readers follow vertical routes to other content instead of reading a text in chronological order. These are invitations to explore aspects further, leading the reader away from the immediate plot, yet augmenting it at the same time. Being steered out of and back into the narrative challenges the reader to recognise that pursuing connections that move away from the plot can substantially enhance her understanding of it. Instead of making readers feel utterly lost in the complex matrix of reading paths, Larsen effectively links the experiences of reading in print and digital formats while adopting an ostensibly non-technological approach. Through mimicking an online reading experience Larsen's novel creates a Brechtian 'Verfremdungseffekt', which focuses the reader's attention on the story as much as on how to read it in order to develop one's own understanding of it. This consequently raises awareness of the reader's own interpretative strategies.

These strategies decode three journeys: T. S.'s inner and outer journey towards maturity and unknown places and the reader's own journey through the dense network of plot and side-plots to meaning on the 'map of the page'. Consequently, this novel has the potential to go beyond reader expectations and teach higher-order thinking, the skills of navigation through a complex network of aspects of a story and subsequently through her own world beyond the confines of the book. This happens when the reader follows and simultaneously moves away from the plot, by 'activating prior knowledge, making predictions and personal connections' as well as engaging with a visualisation of the experience of meaning-making on the pages of the book itself (Ciampa 2012, p. 28).

The place of reading and the reader in immersive virtual environments: Scholastic's *The 39 Clues* series

What is being considered in this second case study are constructions of readers in and expectations readers have of texts that are part of immersive virtual environments. As an example, this case study investigates *The 39 Clues* multi-platform series by Scholastic. The basis for this analysis is the concept of reader participation beyond the long history of children's literature and games that demand active involvement. It focuses on the development that much current children's fiction depends on an interchange between child reader, author, and narrative as 'co-participants in creating [its] meaning' (Dusenberry 2010, p. 443).

Launched in 2008, *The 39 Clues* is the first of Scholastic's three multi-media and multi-platform series produced for readers of 8 to 12 years. Each of these multi-platform series includes books in print and digital form, combined with fully integrated and immersive online games that augment the reading experience. *The 39 Clues* comprises ten printed texts (commissioned books written by seven well-known children's book authors such as Rick Riordan or Peter Lerangis) released periodically; trading cards published periodically in print as well as virtually; and a multifaceted website with online games, blogs and message boards.

This particular series raised the stakes of such initiatives by serialising the books and synchronising the increasing complexity of the immersive online environment with the publication of the books. This wide range of elements provides the 'tools' readers employ in order to find the 39 clues and solve the mystery of the Cahill family. In this respect, the series helps 'extend storytelling beyond the traditional covers of the book' as online players engage with material that tells background stories about characters with images, texts and games (Rich 2008, np). At the same time, reading is portrayed as key to understanding the world around us, to finding one's place, and to making a mark in this world. In this context it is also extended to writing and playing games, emphasising the multitude of ways in which children come across narratives in their lives.

The narrative of *The 39 Clues*, an allusion to John Buchan's adventure spy novel *The Thirty-Nine Steps* (1915), is told partly in print and partly online. In the immersive online environment the boundaries of reality and fiction are blurred on many levels, for example in that the characters are portrayed as living people with frequent staged appearances through photographs, pseudo webpages, blogs, ostensibly real information in newspaper articles, or secret agent reports. At the same time the roles of all involved in the writing, production and reading are blurred. Characters, authors, and readers are referred to as 'agents' and readers become protagonists in the narrative of the quest. What this series therefore highlights is the shifting author–reader dynamic, where online novel communities function as a bridge from print to digital literature and where reader expectations are resisted in that readers are required to become active participants in the quest and cooperate with each other in order to find the clues (Skains 2010, p. 95). As the narrative is part of the immersive virtual environment, it provides a safe space for readers to become an 'active audience' (Hagood 2003, p. 389). Following Dusenberry's conceptualisation, this audience can be defined as 'reader-players' (2010).

Because the series' approach is based on choices for readers in terms of engagement, entry and modes, each linked to a different process of 'reading', the expectation of the reader as being actively engaged is highlighted. In a similar way as Larsen's novel demands readers to make decisions about how to read the novel, *The 39 Clues* offers different paths for and levels of engagement; be it through 'only' reading the fictional stories in the print books, participating in group problem solving, or playing online games, or doing all of the above. Choices have to be made in terms of the order in which the reader 'reads', although '[t]he novels purposefully give the reader the expectation that reading the books comes first, then collecting playing cards, followed by participating in the online community' (Dusenberry 2010, 444–445).

As in Larsen's novel, the reader can call on previous knowledge of the conventions of mystery and detective fiction and the individual elements of the series to gain an enhanced understanding of the narrative. Yet, despite the range of choices, the reader-player does not fully control the meaning-making of the complex network of texts but becomes a 'collaborator-after-the-fact' (Gubar 2009, p. 8). The child reader is 'allowed to exert force on the text's meaning only after the initial limits have been set' by game books that 'privilege certain types of knowledge [...w]hile each game book's effectiveness depends on its ability to negotiate reader-players' expectations' (Dusenberry 2010, p. 445).

Therefore, *The 39 Clues* corroborates reader expectations through its directedness, its sense of denouement and the rationalisation of a mystery. It exceeds these expectations through the necessity to interact with the texts and other readers and through adding the dimension of playing a game on- or offline, for example by offering the prize that can be won as a reward. Media-enhanced children's texts like Scholastic's series expect their readers to create meaningful connections on a range of levels with them. These texts acknowledge and guide the reader-player's expectations, readers have to grasp that these texts depend on a set of rules as well as the narrative, and that the meaning-making of the narrative is influenced by collaboration that builds knowledge collectively (Dusenberry, 2010). Thus 'the differences in the way information is accumulated, shared, and learned, ... are creating profound changes' in the way in which reader-players in such immersive virtual environments read and determine boundaries between reality and fiction (Sekeres and Watson 2011, p. 260).

Transmedia storytelling and the concept of the 'wreader': BradField Productions' Inanimate Alice

The third case study revolves around how readers' expectations and conceptions of readers are redefined in transmedia storytelling that is solely taking place in the digital world. It also exemplifies how the concept of the reader-player is transcended by the forms of engagement offered by the born digital novel *Inanimate*

Alice, created by BradField Productions: writer Kate Pullinger, designer Chris Joseph and producer Ian Harper (2005–2014). This digital novel is 'a multimedia interactive fiction, produced [for reading on screen] using manipulated images, text, games, music and sound effects' (Harper 2010, np). The multimodal narrative encapsulates phenomena of genre blurring, self-referentiality and narrative disruptions, and its conception and reception has as much to do with literature as with literacy. In accordance with Hayles' definition of electronic literature, this pioneering novel 'can be understood as both partaking of literary tradition and introducing crucial transformations that redefine what literature is' (2008, p. 3). At the same time, it reviews the concept of the reader, considering that she becomes a 'wreader' who is as much a producer as she is a consumer of narratives (Landow 1997). The noun 'wreader' combines the terms of 'writer' and 'reader'. It signifies Landow's (1997) concept of the reader as co-producer, where the reader is as much a producer as a reader of a text. Landow developed this concept initially in relation to hypertext-fiction online. Since its creation, the term has been applied to a wider range of aspects of reading-related activities readers engage with in the virtual world, such as writing sequels that are published online, discussing fiction in online communities, adding text and other media to existing digital fiction or producing and sharing their own adaptations of existing multi-media digital fiction. This new type of reader has come about due to the affordances of and easy access to digital technologies which allow 'wreaders' to produce their own episodes of digital fiction and publish them online (http://inanimatealice.info/create/).

The narrative of *Inanimate Alice* echoes themes investigated in connection with *The Selected Works of T. S. Spivet* such as experiencing the world from the perspective of a lonely, dislocated child whose journey is at the same time the journey into adulthood, a 'reading' of the world by creating symbolic visual representations in order to make sense of it, and the young protagonist's increasing agency through the creation of their own means of taking control of their world. Where T. S. uses his old-fashioned drawing tools to design his maps, Alice employs her ba-xi player to create games in which her imaginary friend Brad shows her how to resolve problems in the 'real' world.

Inanimate Alice comprises elements of film, game and literature, yet the narrative continually disrupts the readers' expectations of these genres. In accordance with the findings of the previous case studies, readers' expectations are challenged when narratives in digital and other media build on familiarities that derive from reading print books or familiarity with 'traditional' literary conventions and vice versa. One example is the presentation of the character of Alice, who remains off-screen throughout the episodes, which 'renders this hybrid form of storytelling closer to that of reading a book, where it falls upon the reader to imagine the main character's appearance' (Pullinger 2013, np).

A further subversion occurs as the narrative is partially presented in video format, yet unlike in feature films with a first-person narrative that enable viewers to actually see the protagonist, *Inanimate Alice* subverts this convention as Alice remains off-screen throughout and where her narrative is presented in words on-screen and not as voice-over. It thus creates an enigma that underlines how readers' expectations are challenged by transmedia storytelling.

Disruption of expectations also occurs when the reader in the course of 'reading' *Inanimate Alice* becomes a gamer taking on a 'shooter perspective' that resonates the first person narrative voice of the written words on screen. The reader physically engages with the narrative through touch and sound, moving the plot forward in real time in this process. However, the reader is less in a position to influence the outcome of the story than when playing a conventional videogame as the narrative 'is still linear and episodic [and ...] has already been determined' (O'Rourke 2012, np).

In contrast to the nature of the gameplay in *The 39 Clues*, the gameplay in *Inanimate Alice* is an integral part of and not a departure from the narrative. The gameplay here is not established to emphasise reader choice, as the focus remains on the story that is being told. This gameplay serves a similar purpose to the mapping in Larsen's novel. It slows down the reading process, it focuses readers by engaging them in a different way with aspects of the story. In *Inanimate Alice* the narrator essentially remains the main protagonist, in contrast to the blurring of roles that occurs with the reader-players in *The 39 Clues*. However, Pullinger acknowledges that 'anything that involves interactivity involves a different mindset than reading a piece of fiction' (cited in Pauli 2006, np) and in that sense transmedia storytelling defies expectations that derive from familiarity with genre conventions. At the heart of this subversion of expectations lies the fact that *Inanimate Alice* breaks with traditional reading conventions and demands a multi-faceted and heightened engagement.

This heightened engagement is reflected in the need for the reader to interact with items on the screen that contribute to her understanding of the story. The production team raises awareness of the need to engage physically with the novel at the very beginning of each episode. The introductory paragraph explains how the controls such as computer mouse and sound have to be used to be able to 'read' the story. It clarifies that the reader 'may sometimes need to perform an action for the story to continue' by turning the pages (http://inanimatealice.com/episode3). In the third episode, *Russia*, the ba-xi game involves Brad collecting and saving Matryoshkas. The reader discovers how to work the controls to collect these symbolic figurines, however she also realises that these Matryoshkas have an impact on the outcome of the conflict in the episode. When Alice, who is about to be arrested by a Russian border guard, shows him her ba-xi game and the number of Matryoshkas she has collected, he lets the family go. The episode can only be completed, when the reader has learned how to collect these Matryoshkas herself. This engrosses and at the same time distances the reader, as she is thinking about the story, the meaning of the Matryoshkas and about how to operate the interactive elements, making her aware of herself as a reader as well as the act of reading. This multi-layered engagement in turn augments the process of meaning-making.

Self-referentiality that enhances the experience of reading runs through all aspects of this born digital narrative. The five episodes finished to date contain text and, as in a picturebook, this text tells a story that augments the visual and aural elements. However, these verbal and non-verbal elements, which might remind the reader of a film with subtitles, appear in a non-linear fashion, video screens show similar images running parallel and overlapping each other. Text appears on screen, seems to vanish just in order to reappear briefly, thus drawing specific attention to its purpose and the expectation that readers decode meaning of this resistance to familiar patterns. The reader has to physically press buttons to 'turn pages', mimicking the reading experience of a book and requiring readers to decide when they are ready to move forward.

As regards the gaming aspect of the novel, self-referentiality accentuates the process of growing up. The ludic elements support meaning-making on a meta-level as the reader develops and constructs an understanding of Alice's way of making sense of the world, influencing her own life and the people around her. With each episode the games become more complex as Alice grows older and her skills as a games designer increase. These improved skills allow Alice and the reader to visualise and address creatively more complex aspects of life.

Another dimension of subverting expectations of readers is represented as the reader can become a 'wreader' of *Inanimate Alice*. Here the reader can go beyond 'reading' the individual episodes and engage with the on- and off-site paratexts of the narrative, for example following links to other websites which discuss the novel, which show how the novel was created and where she can go as far as producing her own chapters with free open-source digital tools introduced by the BradField Productions team. These 'wreaders' or co-creators' own episodes, which further blur boundaries between reader and author and provide disruptions of the original episodes' linear plot, augment the narrative by adding novel perspectives and subtexts.

The off-site paratexts of *Inanimate Alice* add disruptions and a layering of meaning. Unlike in self-referential postmodern picturebooks, where the reader is engaged in a conversation about the telling of the story on a meta-level, this meta-level is created in the virtual environment beyond the *Inanimate Alice* website. Part of this environment is the communication that is happening in different places of the world wide web among the community of the novel's creators, co-creators and readers. As Stewart confirms, 'these off-site paratexts … provide an insight into the production processes and shape genre expectations: all of which in turn frame the reception of the text for its readers' (2010, p. 61).

The multiple blurring of boundaries and the subversion of familiar patterns, roles and genre conventions in *Inanimate Alice* portray the subversion of readers' expectations of this born digital narrative. Whereas conceptions of readers are clearly portrayed when attention is drawn to the design of the digital narrative itself, and when the child in *Inanimate Alice* is constructed and constructing at the same time. Consequently, this narrative and its digital environment compose a complex framework for reading and readers on the level of the individual and the community of its 'wreaders'.

Outlook

The narratives examined in the three case studies highlight that expectations of readers in the digital age have as much to do with the grey areas and the blurred boundaries between the different media in which the stories are told as with the readers' previous experiences of reading. The analysis also demonstrates that telling stories across different media does not mean the demise of traditional ways in which young readers read and make meaning of these narratives. On the contrary, story-telling and reading that transcend media significantly enhance the appreciation of literary and other concepts because they add to the awareness of how different media and genres work. Transmedia storytelling also enhances readers' agency as they are encouraged to demonstrate their grasp of these concepts in making deci-sions about their own reading process in the navigation of complex narratives and, in fact, the in production of their own versions of narratives. Therefore, the 'diver-sions in the margin' in Larsen's novel in the form of maps of the un-mappable portray the expectation of readers in the digital age, who are required to make their own choices in what to take into account and what to contradict in their meaning-making process while drawing on personal experiences.

An outlook into future developments underscores that what can transform read-ing and readers' expectations might not be the remediation of printed books in digital format, however advanced this may be. *The 39 Clues* and *Inanimate Alice* exemplify how readers become active participants in virtual environments, real as well as fictional, which expand on the original narrative and offer avenues to engage with or create background stories, new characters and other, also non-fictional, material. We need to understand how diversifying reading practices are changing expectations of readers; and this means we need to recognise that what we have known as boundaries between genres, media, readers and authors are increasingly becoming blurred and that the texts we engage with are becoming more 'slippery' (Fleckenstein 2003, p. 105).

This analysis emphasises that the design of narratives based on digital technolo-gies in one way or another tends to offer readers different points of entry into a text, a wider range of reading paths and the potential to produce and publish their own renditions of these narratives. Thus, the chapter illustrates how the amalgamation of print and digital, of word, sound and image with interactivity in storytelling aug-ments narratives, reader expectations as well as reading practices resulting in a shift that 'requires an additional, non-trivial effort to traverse the text' (De Vivo 2011, pp. 3–4).

Primary sources

Larsen, Reif. *The Selected Works of T. S. Spivet*. London: Random House, 2009.
Pullinger, Kate, Joseph, Chris and Harper, Ian. *Inanimate Alice*, produced by BradField Productions [Online]. 2005–2014. Available at http://www.inanimatealice.com (accessed 7 October 2014).

Pullinger, Kate, Joseph, Chris and Harper, Ian. *Inanimate Alice*, Episode 3: Russia, produced by BradField Productions [Online]. 2005–2014. Available at http://inanimatealice.com/episode3 (accessed 10 July 2014).

Scholastic (2005) *The 39 Clues* [Online]. Available at www.the39clues.com (accessed 10 August 2014).

Secondary sources

Adams, Tim. 'Travels with the Kid Cartographer: In This Much-hyped Debut, a Child Genius Obsessively Maps his Huck Finn-like World. Along the way he Loses Tim Adams', *The Guardian*, 3 May 2009. Available at http://www.guardian.co.uk/books/2009/may/03/reif-larsen-selected-works-ts-spivet (accessed 20 February 2013). Online.

Ciampa, Katia. 'ICANREAD: The Effects of an Online Reading Program on Grade 1 Students' Engagement and Comprehension Strategy Use'. *Journal of Research on Technology in Education (International Society for Technology in Education)*, *45*(1), 27–59, Business Source Complete, EBSCO*host*, viewed 22 May 2015.

De Vivo, Fabio. 'eLiterature: Literature in a Digital Era. Definition, Concept and Status', *elMclip: Research in Electronic Literature*. Available at http://elmcip.net/node/284 (accessed 6 December 2013). 2011. Online.

Dusenberry, Lisa. 'Reader-Players: *The 39 Clues, Cathy's Book*, and the Nintendo DS'. *Children's Literature Association Quarterly*, *35*(4), 443–449. 2010. Print.

Evangelia, Moula. 'Transgressing the Written Literary Norm and Redefining Textness in Contemporary Children's Literature'. E-proceedings of the International Online Language Conference (IOLC), 2, 465–475. 2011. Print.

Fleckenstein, Kristie S. *Embodied Literacies: Imageword and a Poetics of Teaching*. Studies in Writing and Rhetoric. Carbondale, IL: Southern Illinois University Press, 2003. Print.

Gewertz, Catherine. 'Children Still Prefer Print Books to E-Books', *Education Week*, *32*(18), 8–9. 2013. Print.

Gubar, Marah. *Artful Dodgers: Reconceiving the Golden Age of Children's Literature*. Oxford: Oxford University Press, 2009. Print.

Hagood, Margaret C. 'New Media and Online Literacies: No Age Left Behind'. *Reading Research Quarterly*, *38*(3), 387–391. 2003. Print.

Harper, Ian. 'Alice Born Digital: How Transmedia Storytelling Becomes a Billion Dollar Business'. *Publishing Perspectives*, 30 April 2010. Available at http://publishingperspectives.com/2010/04/alice-born-digital-how-transmedia-storytelling-becomes-a-billion-dollar-business (accessed 12 December 2013). Online.

Hayles, N. Katherine. *Electronic Literature: New Horizons for the Literary*. Notre Dame: University of Notre Dame Press, 2008. Print.

Landow, George. *Hypertext 2.0: The Convergence of Contemporary Critical Theory and Technology*. Baltimore, MD: Johns Hopkins University Press, 1997. Print.

Mackey, Margaret. 'At Play on the Borders of the Diegetic: Story Boundaries and Narrative Interpretation'. *Journal of Literacy Research*, *35*(1), 591–632. 2003. Print.

Mackey, Margaret. *Narrative Pleasures in Young Adult Novels, Films and Video Games*. Basingstoke: Palgrave Macmillan, 2011. Print.

O'Rourke, Sophie. 'Inanimate Alice 9 Years Old. How's She Doing?'. *Book Machine*, 21 March 2012. Available at http://bookmachine.org/2012/03/21/inanimate-alice-is-9-years-old-how-is-she-doing (accessed 2 January 2014). Online.

Pauli, Michelle. 'Down with Alice'. *The Guardian*, 7 December 2006. Available at http://www.theguardian.com/books/2006/dec/07/technology.internet (accessed 10 October 2013). Online.

Pullinger, Kate. 'Inanimate Alice: Her Unexpected Rise from Marketing Tool to Pedagogical Blockbuster'. *The Writing Platform*, 13 May 2013. Available at http://www.thewriting platform.com/2013/05/inanimate-alice-her-unexpected-rise-from-marketing-tool-to-pedagogical-blockbuster (accessed 10 September 2013). Online.

Rich, Motoko. 'Using Video Games as Bait to Hook Readers'. *New York Times*, 5 October 2008. Available at http://www.nytimes.com/2008/10/06/books/06games.html?pagewa nted=allandmodule=SearchandmabReward=relbias%3Arand_r=0 (accessed 1 August 2014). Online.

Sekeres, Diane and Watson, Christopher. 'New Literacies and Multimediacy: The Immersive Universe of The 39 Clues'. *Children's Literature in Education*, 42, 256–273. 2011. Print.

Skains, R. Lyle. 'The Shifting Author–Reader Dynamic'. *Convergence: The Journal of Research into New Media Technologies*, 16(1), 95–111. 2010. Print.

Stewart, Gavin. 'The Paratexts of Inanimate Alice: Thresholds, Genre Expectations and Status', *Convergence*, 16, 57–74. 2010. Print.

11

'THIS IS *MY* SHOW!'

Beyond reading to envisioning and enacting

Shirley Brice Heath

In the early eighteenth century, when peddlers' wares included English-language chapbooks, these literary portrayals cast children as villains, adventurers and imaginative creatures who could easily transform themselves into miscreants, thieves and tricksters. Little ones could pose as innocents, drawing attention away from their wily peers who meanwhile deftly parted a wealthy man from his purse. Throughout the eighteenth century, such pictures of children were meant both to entertain little ones and to remind adults of their leadership role, guiding the young to moral and productive pursuits.

Historians of English childhood have examined books and toys created for the young since the end of the eighteenth century (see Hunt, this volume). They have analysed artifacts created for children to identify changing perceptions of children's capacities and roles. These analyses have encouraged the presumption of parents and adults through the ages to believe that their role is to teach the young, passing on skills and knowledge children need as they mature into adulthood. The anthropologist Margaret Mead (1970) labeled this particular process of enculturation 'postfigurative': the young learn primarily from their forebears. Within this view has been a premise that the young not only need but also want the instruction and support that come through discipline, lessons and moral direction from their elders. The Western world's version of postfigurative enculturation reflects Judeo Christian principles and practices asserting that the 'right' written texts provide a vital component of the guidance and discipline children need. Thus children must learn both to read and to value 'proper' books and their sources.

In the second half of the twentieth century, wide reports of child development research told of the extent to which young children were being drawn away from physical activity and imaginative play by new entertainment technologies they could control for themselves. Series books, such as those featuring Olivia the pig by Ian Falconer (*Olivia*, the first book in the series was published in 2000), increasingly portrayed both human children and anthropomorphic animals outpacing adults in taking charge of scenarios from circuses to school plays. By the opening of the twenty-first century, a growing, but still small, share of books written for very young children portrayed enactment of their dreams, fantasies, and creativity. These books featured youngsters devising and managing situations unimaginable to their parents. Some of these featured children reading, and as the century moved on, this reading increasingly accompanied portrayals of individual children creating and acting through their own creative projects of art and science.

During this same period, prevailing beliefs about children and what they need to enter adulthood shifted away from human agents as guides toward technology as agency and source for information, social company, and development of knowledge about the world. Mead predicted this shift as early as 1970, when she outlined the 'prefigurative' world of enculturation that would characterise the future. She maintained that the pace of cultural change and need to stay open to the future would force adults to have to learn from their children as well as their forebears. In addition, to some extent, both parents and children would take part in 'co-figurative' enculturation, learning from their peers in addition to their ancestors.

Mead asserted the need to give up expectations that post-figurative enculturation could take humans into the future. In a prefigurative world, children would always learn faster and in more ways than their elders. Children would gain skills and content unknown and often invisible and unpredictable to adults. Moreover, the young would then acquire expertise and information in ways far more varied than their parents. The experience, range of skills and modes of learning of the young were sure to stretch beyond what those of prior generations could know, do, or might even value. As a consequence, Mead cautioned that adults of the prefigurative future must 'teach their children not what to learn, but *how to learn* and not what they should be committed to, but *the value of commitment*' (emphasis not in the original, 1970, p. 72).

This chapter considers ways in which books published after 2010 picture youngsters demonstrating how they integrate reading into their choice of pursuits. In these books, authors and illustrators portray children creating, building and dancing while bewildered adults observe and listen. The children of these texts and illustrations put into practice principles of learning that neuroscientists and developmentalists identify as critical if the brain's potential is not to be curtailed through parents' over-reliance on technological devices during children's early development. When adults celebrate their young children's facility with devices such as iPads, mobile phones and computers, they fail to consider what children are *not* doing while they respond to the entertaining appeal of what comes from swipes, taps, and button-pushing. Young children's imagination does not easily go to the intrigue of what lies behind and outside the technology of the moment. Mead would point out to those parents living out her predictions for prefigurative enculturation that children following technologies' push-me touch-me seduction rarely think beyond the immediate gratification of entertainment. Children's adeptness in making technology give them exactly what they want when they want it blinds adults to considering Mead's cautions surrounding the critical importance of teaching children *how to learn* as well as *how to value commitment.*

Technological changes

What Margaret Mead could not have predicted within her theories surrounding prefigurative learning was the dizzying speed of technological change that would bring about unforeseen alterations in not only valuation but also processes of *what to learn.* By the end of the first decade of the twenty-first century, almost all knowledge rested literally just beneath one's fingertips by way of the Internet.

Thus children (and many parents) came to see little or no point in the insistence of school curricula on memorisation of facts and figures. Testing for this kind of knowledge within strict limits of time for exam completion increasingly drew public questioning of this kind of 'accountability'. Retrieval is what counts, or so the thinking of state schools and many parents went. Efforts accelerated to put iPads, mobile phones and computers into the hands of children at younger and younger ages. Educators and policymakers as well as corporate spokespersons argued that the future of young children's career development depended on their learning through typing, swiping and talking to various technologies. Schools and towns closed their libraries. Schools stopped teaching handwriting, music, drawing and drama. Mead's view of prefigurative enculturation seemed to be evident in every home and school where adults readily bragged that their children now knew far more than their elders would ever know about how to get the most out of technologies of all kinds.

Meanwhile, far away from primary schools and town council meetings, a different kind of technological advancement was taking place in the world of neuroscience research. After 2010, functional magnetic resonance imaging (fMRI) technologies provided neuroscientists means of examining how different sections of the brain work in synchrony and how neural dedication to particular types of tasks becomes established during childhood and adolescence. These scientists could now deepen their understanding of ways that certain activities and environmental factors shape how and what children observe, imitate, imagine, store in memory and use to form their aspirations and self-perceptions. Scientists could now view what happens in the brain during the *haptic learning* that derives from touching or gaining information through the 'eyes of the skin', particularly of the hands and forearms, as well as the fingers when they work as the extended tools of hands and arms (Pallasmaa 2009, 2012). Taking part in the arts, especially music, drawing, dance and drama, gives children practice in developing their haptic understanding, which in turn advances aspects of perception, language processing and conceptual representation (see Chapter 4 of Wilson 1998, for example, on the hands at work in puppetry and dramatic play and Chapter 10 on the haptic learning of musicians).

With fMRI technologies, neuroscientists can study what happens to visual images in the brain of a child gripping a tool during creative production or performance. Children receive haptic or hand-guided feedback whenever they grip an instrument such as pencil, paintbrush, bow or neck of a violin, viola or cello. This process enhances the act of mentally visualising what lies beyond the current moment of action. Gripping with the hand sends what neurologists call 'force patterns' to portions of the brain that enable individuals to envision what lies ahead (Reiner 2000, 2008). As children learn to verbalise the sense of 'nextness' they receive when gripping objects in their hand, they learn to think before they act. The question "What am I to do now that I have this object in my grip?" becomes operative as children mature beyond their own initial assumptions about possible actions to take with gripped objects.

With maturation comes children's increasing competence in verbal expression of their imagined possibilities of what they can do with materials as they draw, build, dance and act. Haptic learning draws children toward increasingly complex powers of seeing and interpreting. Guided practice is essential, however, for the young to continue to improve visual as well as auditory perception of multi-layered details. Doing so often has to take place in the midst of seeming chaos – different kinds of messages and signals coming from peers, adults, and children's own dreams and imaginations. By 2014, neuroscientists were learning about behavioural and neural correlates of what came to be termed 'executive functioning' (EF). A collection of cognitive capacities, EF includes the ability to plan and self-monitor. The neural correlates of EF also affect children's competence in rule representation, cognitive flexibility and the mental control necessary to switch tasks without becoming confused. Musical training, with piano and strings, in particular, enhances EF, which in turn correlates with both verbal fluency and language processing speed of children (Zuk, Benjamin, Kenyon, and Gaab 2014).

As youngsters produce and create projects in either the arts or sciences, they literally 'feel' themselves as agents or builders who make things happen. However, they can do so only as they gain practice and ideally encouragement in listening, observing, envisioning and then enacting or dramatising their internal images and scenarios. This internal envisioning benefits from interests that lead children to spend hours in activities that force them to discern slight differences in features of the shape and orientation of small objects, such as Lego pieces, dollhouse furnishings and jigsaw puzzle pieces. The same point applies to listening in order to sort out acoustic regularities. Perceptual abilities advance as children sort out regularities of sounds and their contexts to predict what might come next. Through both practice and modeling of visual, auditory and tactile discernment as well as cognitive categorisation, young learners reduce the number of struggles the cognitive system faces in sorting irrelevant from relevant or pertinent cues (Grill-Spector, Henson, and Martin 2006).

What then about reading books?

Does reading with adults make a difference in young children's creativity and sense of agency? Does the handling of books, turning of pages and flipping here and there through a book to locate a particular imagine do the same? Some argue that technologies make text and image easily available to children. What then is so different about picturebooks? Do such books and the time they capture with adults during reading teach children *how to learn* and to undertake commitments to positive values and activities?

An initial obvious difference between picturebooks and technologies is the permanence and immediate retrievability of image and text in picturebooks. Flipping back to prior pages, finding the same book in the same slot in the bookcase, and discerning differences in detail from covers to inside pages ensures a variety of forearm and hand movements, along with pointing to objects and their features. The fact that images 'stand still' and remain retrievable enables body movement of several types: running back to the bookcase to find a particular book, turning pages to locate a certain animal or bird and pulling out inserts and pop-up sections of books (see Wolpert and Styles, this volume).

A second immediate difference between technologies and picturebooks is the invitation books give to children and adults of reading *together*. In this collaboration, the two look, talk, sound out emotions and actions pictured and take control of interpretive routes. *Directed talk* encircles adult and child during picturebook reading. Since 2010, child language research has shown the advantages to both language acquisition and processing of language that is directed to children over that which takes place in the ambient environment (Weisleder and Fernald 2013). When eye contact and face-to-face alignment accompany talk to children, their comprehension and production of language increase. Within picturebook reading, deictic or pointing gestures by both child and adult go along with talk, creating a complex of stimuli that young children from early toddlerhood can imitate and adapt. The simultaneity of gesture, facial orientation, visual gaze, talk and image makes a memorable and often emotional impression on young children. Their frequent requests to 'read it again' indicate their readiness to take in multiple forms of direction and directness at the same time. Moreover picturebooks compel interpretation, comparison and contrast, and exploration of possibilities not explicitly addressed in pictures and text of these books. These interpretive chats between parent reader and child listener inspire imaginative jaunts as well as activities that can go on well outside the covers and contexts of picturebooks.

Beyond the reading process, the content of picturebooks published since 2010 gives further evidence of how some of these books put into place findings from child development and neuroscience research. In the picturebooks described below, children engage in creative work and play leading to innovation and invention. Underlying this sampling choice is the premise that authors and illustrators of the books chosen have absorbed from the popular press neuroscience findings that relate to brain development in early childhood. In addition, artists who work in the world of children's books are regularly featured at conferences on literacy that stress the extent to which neuroscience research findings sharply contradict directions of change undertaken in testing and curricular programmes as well as national education reform policies. For decades, artists have reflected in their works for children contradictions to the rigidly normative. Classics in children's literature routinely get rid of parents, put children in control of their lives, and illustrate the sense and sensibilities of the young, as well as the draw of the 'forbidden' offered by books (see Smith, this volume).

In findings from neuroscientists, artists see much of their own thinking vindicated, and it would be naïve not to expect them to use their creative works to celebrate these ways of thinking. Cognitive neuroscience makes evident the importance to brain development of performative learning that engages senses of seeing, hearing and touching as well as the rewards from precision with hand and forearm manoeuvres. Simultaneous engagement of the emotions in any expression of creativity enhances learning, memory and self-awareness (Damasio 2008). Artists and children, whether engaged in visual, literary, dramatic or any other performative mode of expression, envision their work as it takes shape in their head, heart and through their hands. Both artists and children 'map' in their heads as well as their sketches what they have done, think now, and project ahead (see Warnecke, this volume).

The books noted below for brief analysis reflect artists at work in partnership with children and also, whether knowingly or not, with ongoing findings from cognitive neuroscience. Moreover, these books portray ways that children's past experiences with reading (maps, books and notebooks) influence their process of bringing imagination into action.

Rosie Revere, Engineer (Beaty and Roberts 2013) tells in verse the story of a shy girl who dares not speak in her classroom. But at night when no one is looking, she takes 'found' objects and builds, making 'gadgets and gizmos'. When her engineering works are discovered and laughed at by adults, Rosie vows silence and secrecy. One day, however, a great-great aunt comes to visit. She has spent her career building airplanes. A bond between the two engineers, one young, one old, is sealed when the aunt tells Rosie that the "only thrill left on her list is to fly". The rest is predictable, for Rosie determines to build a 'gizmo' that will help her aunt fly. She does so, but when she invites her aunt to watch, Rosie's helicopter flies for a bit and then crashes. Her aunt is delighted, telling Rosie that she has done what she set out to do: build a flying machine. Never mind that it crashed, for this failure was a first try, 'a brilliant first flop' that was a 'raging success!' Rosie's aunt then gives her a notebook in which she has sketched the design of early flying machines, many of which failed, but their 'success' was in their leading to production of some of the familiar 'flying machines' from Boeing and other engineering firms in which the aunt had worked. Rosie studies the notebook and returns to school, no longer shy but now filled with ideas of 'gizmos and gadgets and doohickeys' and determination that she and her classmates must try to engineer. She has a new role to play, now knowing from her notebook and her experience that 'perfect failures' are sure to come on any route to 'raging successes'.

Rosie Revere, Engineer followed the highly successful 2007 volume *Iggy Peck, Architect* by the same author and illustrator (Beaty and Roberts 2007). The boy Iggy has a passion for building from any substance into any structure. When he reaches his second year of school, however, his teacher declares that no building is to be done – only reading, writing and arithmetic. A class picnic to an island gives Iggy and classmates the chance they need to demonstrate the merits of building. The footbridge to the island collapses, the teacher faints and the children build from boots, tree roots and string a temporary bridge that saves the day and convinces their teacher that worse things than spending time 'building a dream' could occupy young children.

Both of these books give ample evidence of the power of children's imagination, use of their hands and heads in new roles and, most dramatically, their ability to remember written source materials and to observe materials in their environment to size up their potential use in an envisioned project. These books underline the power of mathematics and reading in several ways. The covers and end papers of both books, as well as some pages within the text, use graph paper as background. Models, sketches, and calculations are scribbled here and there throughout the text as the children take up their projects.

The theme of linking a grasp of abstract concepts to concrete activities and assumed roles persists in books that portray children in their role of enculturating adults prefiguratively while demonstrating and explaining to their elders what is happening and what yet needs to happen. Children draw, read, build models and create while they explain, looking up often to see if adults are indeed listening and watching. *If I Built a House* (Van Dusen 2012) allows Jack, a young imaginative builder, to introduce his sceptical mother to the dream house he has planned. Robots, techniques of water conservation, rooms for sculpting and drawing, along with gravity-free rooms constitute his dream house. Jack thinks beyond his mother as well as other adult doubters. 'Design' is what counts, according to Jack, and to ensure a place for design, any dream house Jack builds will have a 'plexiglas playroom' that puts play at the centre of the world of activities in Jack's house.

Play is mother to the arts. *Frances Dean Who Loved to Dance and Dance* (Sif 2014) tells the story of a little girl whose love of dancing takes her into the outdoor world where birds are her only audience. But she feels she cannot dance elsewhere with her hair in tangles, arms askew, and legs and feet bouncing and pounding. She soon forgets how to dance. Then she comes across a girl, younger than she, who sits on a park bench singing. Frances Dean joins in. That evening she cannot sleep because she remembers the joy the girl's singing gave her. Frances Dean wonders what could happen if she dared to share her dancing with others. She dances, first with the birds, then with 'the old lady in the square', and later with the young singer who has the lyrics stored in memory. Together the two girls take their singing and dancing throughout the park to not only the birds, but also to mothers and children, bicyclists, sunbathers and picnickers. The play of their improvisations works magic for all.

Tricking parents into co-learning is another feature of notable picturebooks. *One Cool Friend* (Buzzeo and Small 2012) tells the story of Elliot, a nerdy young boy who agrees to go to the zoo with his absent-minded father. The request "May I have a penguin?" leads his father to think Elliot is referring to a stuffed toy, whereas Elliot, a young scientist, takes home a live penguin. Elliot learns and adapts to the needs of his penguin. References to reading, geographical knowledge, and an understanding of the habits of penguins who come from another continent demonstrate that project work, play and 'planful' negotiation work very well in the hands and minds of children. All this new knowledge threatens to overwhelm Elliot's father. Meanwhile, Elliot busily creates new contexts he could never before have imagined. The antics of the penguin go a long way toward altering plans and calling for new knowledge, skills and ideas on the part of both father and son.

How to Bake a Book, originally published in the United Kingdom in 2014 (Burfoot), sets up a lone child, a female character that relies on her 'weigh[ing] out the words' as she 'bakes a cake'. She measures and counts, thinking all the while of what else her project needs. She uses her prior knowledge of books to guide her as she 'bakes'. She decides that emotional content words must come first. Then the little baker chooses to add some words that reflect in their sound the actions they portray: *gurgle*, *squelch*, and *splosh*. Patience is called for in the little girl's creation of characters who work to make the plot 'thicken'. The final touch comes, of course, in the addition of punctuation as well as calibration of the necessary quantity of 'happiness glaze' for the book that is to be baked.

In all these books, children take on roles beyond that of child or student, even in the face of setbacks such as silence, rejection or ridicule from adults. Children devise projects that reflect creative differences. As they do so, they use their hands and forearms to build, draw, repair, write and perform. The passage of time in these books reveals the extent to which children's conceptual memory is highly interdependent with their prior reading and knowledge of books as well as their physical, sensory and emotional interactions with others as they embody their own projects (Gibbs 2005). Immediate interpretation of concepts, as well as their long-term memory, shows the children relying on what neuroscientists term 'represented features' whose details can be visually detected only through close visual attention as well as trial and error and ongoing emotional connection or commitment. Concepts are represented in the brain through distributed cortical cell arrays or assemblies. Thus when young children acquire and develop concepts, abstract and concrete, they do so through actions that cut across motor, sensory and emotional connections in the brain (Kiefer and Pulvermüller 2012).

The so-what question

Readers of this chapter will and should ask "so what does this tell us about children's reading in the digital age?" Within this question is the matter of how illustrative in the world of children's book publishing since 2010 are the books analysed here? With what frequency are these ideas reflected within recent works of literature produced in English for young children in the United Kingdom, Australia, New Zealand, Canada and the United States? The short answer has to be "not often enough".

The reality is that publishers in the English-speaking world have since 2010 presented only a relative minority of publications that feature children at work in roles and performances in which they apply what they have learned from reading and from life experience. Even fewer publications portray children using their hands and forearms to express themselves and to execute projects. The majority of books published for young children since 2010 feature anthropomorphised animals or objects (such as crayons, cars, buses and houses) as central characters. Books in which human children carry action and plot appear far less frequently. Furthermore, in the majority of these books, children undertake adventures that bring them into competitions in which they must use advanced technologies of various types in order to escape or to win out over competitors.

Moreover, among those books published after 2010 that featured children as central characters, only a small proportion portray children busily planning, creating and performing. A substantial portion of these picturebooks and early reading books have placed children in some relationship to one or more technologies – often either automotive or communicative. In these plots, children react to events through and with these technologies rather than create and connect with other children and with adults. In contrast to the books summarised in this chapter, those that feature children in the context of recent technologies rarely emphasise children's own creative 'hand and head work' of referring to the books, maps and drawings created by others or through their own sketching, designing and building within adult-like roles.

Where the neuroscience research points

A key issue raised by neuroscience research in relation to reading and technology has been the loss of three aspects of childhood. The most prominent loss has been exploratory and imaginative play children carry out *with* adults who serve as attentive engaged partners. Neuroscientists and developmentalists increasingly point to the hazards of closing off opportunities for children's free play (Brown and Vaughan 2009). As children spend more of their time alone captured in passive spectatorship before the entertainment traps of technologies such as game consoles, iPads and mobile phones, they lose out on more than the joy and fulfilment that creative joint play brings.

A second significant loss to childhood has come in the sharp decline in opportunities for children to explore freely the outdoor world of nature (Louv 2008). 'Stranger danger' fears keep children indoors much of their time or under the supervision of 'intimate strangers', such as coaches, camp counsellors and instructors in a range of organised pursuits. Numerous fears about 'what might happen', along with the increase in two-working-parent families, lead parents to organise their children's out-of-school life by scheduling their time. Under the supervision of 'intimate strangers', children take part in pre-scripted rule-governed activities such as sports. Creative open-ended activities or back-referencing to reading or drawing have little place in team sports, games and tournaments of competition.

A third concern raised in cognitive neuroscience research relates to the loss of children's opportunities to experiment in the arts with all types of art supplies, tools and materials for building projects, and open-ended toys such as blocks. Only within open-ended arts programmes led by artists who inspire and encourage children to 'go where your imagination takes you' can children spend hours working unfettered with a range of materials and tools and reading, observing and listening with adults who think, talk about and demonstrate these arts (Heath 2012). As schools replace pencils, paintbrushes and finger paints with iPads and keyboards, children no longer learn to write by hand or to use cursive script (James and Engelhardt 2012). Because of the particular type of grip that holding instruments of sketching, drawing and painting entails, this particular loss appears to be correlated with children's decline in capacity for sustained attentiveness and long-term memory retention. A key aspect of evolution as a higher-order primate has been dependence on hands and forearms for exploring and managing the physical world. Thus movement of both in the service of creating as well as grasping and wielding has become key to linguistic performance and conceptual processing in human behaviours.

Neuroscience studies consistently show that children's grasp of both concrete and abstract concepts depends on representing these concepts in both sensory and motor areas of the brain. Moreover, context matters in such processing, and modes of play in nature, with creative arts, and in enacted roles enable children to imagine, create, modify and remember these contexts. They do so first in their imagination and planning and subsequently in their lived experience when they actually execute and embody plans built through conceptual processing.

The way ahead?

No one can claim that books such as those analysed here reach more than a slim minority of children in the Anglo world of children's books. Research that relies primarily on observation grows less and less useful for generalisations surrounding ubiquitous behaviours such as reading or writing. As a consequence, scholars must sharply delimit any conclusions they draw from observing the behaviours of only a relatively few individuals. This is the case when scholars try to generalise about literacy behaviours. The rapid population explosion and global expansion of technologies to the far corners of the world within the second half of the twentieth century have made it impossible to collect either valid or reliable data on questions critical to reading patterns and values of either children or adults. The wide span of instruments and sources for reading in English include printed image-rich texts as only one of many modes.

Thus scholars cannot monitor use of all the devices for reading in order to document who reads what, how and with what level of retention of content. Therefore, quantitative conclusions surrounding whether or not technologies have stimulated and expanded reading or reduced it in volume and extent amount to little more than guesswork. We do not yet have the means of tracing behavioural patterns for massive numbers of individuals who seem in some contexts to be reading all the time by one means or another. Therefore, we would do well to remember that data on which chapters of this volume are based stick closely to artifactual materials (such as books) and qualitative portrayals of observed and self-reported reading patterns of a relatively small number of children (and young adults) engaging with a range of technologies that convey English-language texts in modern economies.

In these economies, factors beyond preferences that children may have for books of certain types influence publishers and authors in turn. Research findings from child developmentalists or neuroscientists are regarded as irrelevant by publishers that have particular markets they want to reach. Authors and illustrators whose publishers have close ties with school policies and practices will ignore research findings that could support production of texts and illustrations unacceptable to schools and particular segments of the population. For example, picturebooks such as those summarised in this chapter are most likely to appeal to parents and teachers ready to tolerate the imaginative antics inspired by Rosie, Frances Dean, Elliot, and other characters who want to build, act, draw, sing, dance or bring home a penguin.

Yet, search engines and the general press are likely to continue their reporting of child development, pediatric neuroscience and learning sciences research. In the coming years, findings from this research will move with increasing speed and force into the mind of the greater public who may bring to the attention of education policymakers and publishers research findings and their implications. As this happens, authors and illustrators of children's books will find profit in following where the research points and the sales go. Within a year of its publication, *Rosie Revere, Engineer* reached the best-seller list in the United States, and it was often the only book among the top ten that featured a human child as key character. Moreover, the subtle weaving and layering of science-and-art-related themes into text and image present the kind of challenge artists relish. These themes, moreover, underscore what artists, close observers of childhood, have seen in the world of children free of the leash of technologies of entertainment.

A final point regarding the books discussed here as well as others that are similar must be noted. These books almost never feature children playing, thinking and working together in small groups as was a predominant pattern of books written for young readers in the late twentieth century (for example, see the *Friends Forever* series and the trio of books in *The Mysterious Benedict Society* series). Instead, all books noted in this chapter centre on one child, an individual innovator, planner and leader who often reads, consults maps and refers to sketches and plans. This reflection of individual initiative and creative thinking matches ideals of inquisitive individualism often held by the mainstream parents who are most likely to purchase and read these books. Moreover, schools increasingly stress individual work, and the Anglo world continues to celebrate individuals who strike out on their own to explore, innovate, create and design.

Individual characters featured in books as well as films related to these books remain in the heads of youngsters who seek in numerous ways to imitate and re-enact independently creative girls and boys. When characters take up activities and represent skills available to young children, such as drawing, reading, building, dancing or singing, youngsters are inspired to do the same. As they assume these roles, their readiness to *take* centre stage over adults thrives.

Lily, a three-year old who watched the DVD of *Frozen*, listened to the music and repeatedly searched illustrations in books associated with the Disney film. One day she asked her father to play the film's music on the piano. When he bought the music, set it before him on the piano, and began to pick out the notes, the familiar melody of the song "Let it go" emerged. He began to sing and Lily joined him in singing as she climbed up beside her father on the piano bench. She tentatively fingered the keys as he played and sang. Shortly, Lily looked up at her father with a firm set to her jaw: "Daddy, you don't sing". He protested, "But I want to sing". Pushing her shoulders back, she eyed him directly and announced, "Daddy, this is *my* show".

Stories such as Lily's should assure those who fear the replacement of books by technologies of entertainment. Picturebooks, in particular, remain safe, protected by artistic merits and interpretive openness. Their best security, however, comes in their insistence that adults and children read and talk together, making '*my show*' imperatives sure to keep Mead's prefigurative enculturation alive.

Primary sources

Beaty, Andrea. *Iggy Peck, Architect*. David Roberts, illustrator. New York: Abrams, 2007.

Beaty, Andrea. *Rosie Revere, Engineer*. David Roberts, illustrator. New York: Abrams, 2013.

Burfoot, Ella. *How to Bake a Book*. London: Macmillan Books, 2014.

Buzzeo, Toni. *One Cool Friend*. David Small, illustrator. New York: Penguin, 2012.

Falconer, Ian. *Olivia*. New York: Simon & Schuster, 2000.

Sif, Birgitta. *Frances Dean Who Loved to Dance and Dance*. (Originally published in Sweden). Somerville, MA: Candlewick Press, 2014.

Van Dusen, Chris. *If I Built a House*. New York: Penguin, 2012.

Secondary sources

Brown, Stuart and Vaughan, Christopher. *Play: How it Shapes the Brain, Opens the Imagination, and Invigorates the Soul*. New York: Penguin, 2009. Print.

Damasio, Antonio. *Descartes' Error: Emotion, Reason and the Human Brain*. New York: Random House, 2008. Print.

Gibbs, Raymond, Jr. *Embodiment and Human Cognition*. Cambridge, MA: MIT Press, 2005. Print.

Grill-Spector, K., Henson, R., and Martin A. Repetition and the Brain: Neural Models of Stimulus-specific Effects. *Trends in Cognitive Science*, 10, 14–23. 2006.

Heath, Shirley Brice. *Words at Work and Play: Three Decades in Family and Community Life*. Cambridge, UK: Cambridge University Press, 2012. Print.

James, Karin H. and Engelhardt, Laura. The Effects of Handwriting Experience on Functional Brain Development of Pre-Literate Children. *Trends in Neuroscience and Education*, 1(1), 32–42. 2012. Print.

Kiefer, Markus and Pulvermüller, Friedemann. Conceptual Representations in Mind and Brain: Theoretical Developments, Current Evidence and Future Directions. *Cortex, 48,* 805–825. 2012. Print.

Louv, Richard. *Last Child in the Woods: Saving our Children from Nature-deficit Disorder.* Chapel Hill, NC: Algonquin Press, 2008. Print.

Mead, Margaret. *Culture and Commitment: A Study of the Generation Gap.* New York: Doubleday, 1970. Print.

Pallasmaa, Juhani. *The Eyes of the Skin: Architecture and the Senses.* New York: Wiley, 2012. Print.

Pallasmaa, Juhani. *The Thinking Hand.* New York: Wiley, 2009. Print.

Reiner, Miriam. The Validity and Consistency of Force Feedback Interfaces in Telesurgery. *Journal of Computer-aided Surgery, 9,* 69–74. 2008. Print.

Reiner, Miriam. The Nature and Development of Visualization: A Review of What is Known. In *Visualization: Theory and Practice in Science Education* (pp. 25–29), Eds. J. K. Gilbert, M. Reiner, and M. Nakhleh. Surrey, UK: Springer, 2000. Print.

Weisleder, Adriana and Fernald, Anne. (2013). Talking to Children Matters: Early Language Experience Strengthens Processing and Builds Vocabulary. *Psychological Science, 24*(11), 2143–2152. 2013. Print.

Wilson, Frank R. *The Hand: How Its Use Shapes the brain, Language, and Human Culture.* New York: Vintage Press, 1998. Print.

Zuk, J., Benjamin C., Kenyon A., Gaab N. Behavioral and Neural Correlates of Executive Functioning in Musicians and Non-Musicians. *PLoS ONE, 9*(6): e99868. 2014. doi:10.1371/journal.pone.0099868. Online.

AUTHORS AND BOOK TITLES INDEX

SUBJECT INDEX

CPSIA information can be obtained
at www.ICGtesting.com
Printed in the USA
BVHW04s1642160818
524700BV00001B/2/P